In Praise of *Results Stat!*

"As someone who has studied not just Disney but experiences the world over, no one captures the nuts-and-bolts of creating a world-class 'wow' experience like Mark David Jones. And I so love that he focuses here on the healthcare industry, for research shows that the better the patient experience, the better the outcomes. And that's what truly matters in healthcare. So read *Results Stat!* and follow its tools and prescriptions to transform both the patient and the caregiver experience to be magical. Now."

– B. JOSEPH PINE II, coauthor, *The Experience Economy: Competing for Customer Time, Attention, and Money*

"What an amazing book! It is like having a mentor and coach to get us all from the page to action. Exceptional customer care in healthcare isn't just a service — it's an experience that people will remember for the rest of their lives, or until their next interaction with your organization. This guide offers a comprehensive roadmap, providing practical insights, real-world examples and templates from Mark David Jones' long career with top global organizations for implementing empathetic processes seamlessly. *Results Stat!* is an indispensable resource for organizations navigating change by fostering meaningful and compassionate staff and patient engagement"

— SUE KONG, Director, NHS Elect, National Health Service UK

"*Results Stat!* by Mark David Jones is a masterful blend of leadership wisdom that effectively translates the operational excellence of Disney into actionable strategies for the healthcare industry. As a former Disney executive who led Epcot and now as CEO of a nationwide behavioral health company, I can attest to the unique insights this book provides. It is essential for enhancing team collaboration, patient experience, and operational success in any healthcare setting. I highly recommend this book to all healthcare professionals who aspire to integrate the best of Disney's innovations to create outstanding healthcare outcomes. Mark's guidance ensures that every reader can use these tools to achieve significant improvements in their organizations."

— BRAD REX, President and CEO, eHome Counseling Group

"Our current healthcare landscape is mired with highly charged, fast-paced, and rapidly evolving chaos and uncertainty requiring leaders at all levels to more effectively engage their teams in creative problem solving to improve operational outcomes. In his book *Results Stat!*, Mark David Jones lays out a clear approach and process, coupled with practical tools and solutions, to support any healthcare leader to enact change effectively and implement improvement initiatives with their team."

Using relevant, relatable healthcare examples, this book is brimming with tried and tested 'Pro Tips', tools, templates, and self-exams that are grounded in Mark's own experiences working with world-class organizations. He skillfully demonstrates how to apply these principles to achieve success in improving both team engagement and the patient experience. It's like having a personal coach at your disposal to guide you step-by-step through any change or improvement effort!"

— SHREYSHREE RAJA, Former Director, Leadership & Organizational Development, Mount Sinai Hospital and St Michael's Hospital, Toronto, Ontario, Canada

Rx
RESULTS
STAT!
Proven World-Class Tools
To Liberate Your Healthcare Team
MD: Jones Signature:
MARK DAVID JONES

Results Stat! Proven World-Class Tools to Liberate Your Healthcare Team
By Mark David Jones

Proudly AI-Free Content: Absolutely no AI was used in the production of this book content.

Publisher: Highpoint Business Resources Press — HBRPress.com
Copy Editor: Caroline Coppel
Cover and Interior Design: Oncore Strategy

ISBN 978-0-9788929-0-6 (softcover)
ISBN 978-0-9788929-1-3 (eBook)
ISBN 978-0-9788929-2-0 (audio book)

Library of Congress Control Number: 2024909633

Dedication

To all my cherished family, friends, colleagues, and clients — without whom this book would have been finished *eight years earlier.*

Yes, this is that kind of book.
Prepare for some truth...and tools to make your life better!

With Sincere Appreciation

These acknowledgements typically are at the end of the book, but I want to put them front and center, where they belong:

First, to the late Fred Lee — who (easily) convinced me to partner with him on this implementation resource. His best-selling book, *If Disney Ran Your Hospital,* touched hundreds of thousands of healthcare professionals. His life touched even more. I've made every effort to ensure his confidence in my organizational transformation expertise is reflected in these pages. To know Fred and his effervescent wife Aura, is to be inspired. He made — and continues to make, through his book — a difference. Rest in peace, friend.

To my delightful, beautiful, talented, and beloved wife, Emma — you simply make everything ...better. I thank God for placing you in my life and being my (much) better half (according to everyone). Thank you for supporting my crusade to rescue healthcare and the heroes that are called to serve. I cherish how you inspire me every day. (That's how we roll, eh?) *Wo hao ai ni!*

In addition, I appreciate the scores of family members, friends, colleagues, and clients that buoyed me throughout this process. I am deeply thankful for your support, insights, feedback, and patience during the years (and years) it took to finish this book. Our shared "tribe" will *always* be a precious thing to me.

Of course, no professional book comes about without the talents of editing and design pros. My meticulous editor Caroline Coppel and adept designers Keith & Dana Sherrer from Oncore Strategy are expertly talented and extraordinary people. It was a pleasure collaborating with you!

Finally, to you the reader. You, and those you care for, are the reason this book exists. The thousands of hours of research and writing/re-writing was done to create a clear way for you and your team to optimize your potential and fulfill the reason you joined the healthcare profession. Please share whatever you find of value with others in your industry so, together, we can elevate healthcare to where it belongs: Providing remarkable and compassionate care to all those in need. By *adapting* these best practices of world-class organizations, your hopes are undeniably attainable. Your efforts to implement these proven strategies and tools will make a difference on what — and who — matters most! I'm proud to partner with you on this adventure!

Mark David Jones

Contents

SECTION FOUR

Prepare Your Outcomes

SECTION FIVE

Secure Your Future

SECTION ONE

Why This Matters (and Why It Works)

1

Purpose of this Implementation Book

Why write a Change Implementation Book for Healthcare? The healthcare industry has experienced seismic changes—and the chaos continues.

Your clinical operation faces unprecedented instability, with ongoing challenges to staff and patients.

Your team is frustrated, struggling to deliver the personal care that your patients so desperately need. Facing external problems you didn't create.

And you—you got into healthcare with a passion to make a difference.

And you know it shouldn't be this difficult!

Imagine if there was a one-stop resource with proven solutions, used by the most successful companies, that make it easier for you and your team to overcome all these challenges and deliver consistent, world-class care.

Imagine if you could gain insights directly from an implementation leader who has personally led numerous successful operational improvement efforts in healthcare organizations like yours.

Well, you don't have to imagine it. This book was written to provide practical tools to improve your leadership, team engagement, patient satisfaction, and outcomes—both clinical and operational.

This book was created to help you and your team make it easier to provide the quality care you *know* you can provide—by implementing improvements you *know* are possible.

Giving you the tools to lead them from mayhem to mastery (and a more satisfying work life).

You have sacrificed so much to help others. You deserve help to succeed.

And, quite frankly, I have the experience, the desire, and the ability to help.

So, I'm damn well going to.

Period.

It's as simple as that.

The Catalyst for Results, Stat!

So, what was the impetus for this healthcare implementation book?

When Fred Lee wrote *If Disney Ran Your Hospital: 9 ½ Things You Would Do Differently* in 2004, he told me he never imagined it would become the best-selling healthcare leadership book in history. Fred once mentioned that he simply wanted to introduce healthcare professionals to a better approach that he and I discussed when we were at Disney World together (for the remainder of this book, I'll be referring to the Disney Company as simply "Disney"). With well over 500,000 copies in print (and published in five languages), it is a testimony to the substantial need to put the "*care* back in healthcare"—and doing so based on strategies from a company that is consistently growing by engaging those they serve. The purpose of this book is to provide the tactics that can bring those strategies to life in your organization, based on far more than just the tools Disney uses.

My story with Fred began as part of the team that brought him to the Disney Institute. I was co-lead for the project to design a program to apply the Disney approach to the healthcare profession because of my previous experience in healthcare. We asked Fred to join us to add "industry confirmation" to our program. Fred provided many examples of how the Disney approach could elevate any healthcare operation. The program was a success for years after Fred left to write his book, but I grew increasingly frustrated by not being able to share a more detailed implementation consultation, because of the limitations that Disney's legal department imposed. Upon retiring from Disney after leading numerous operational transformation efforts, I was eager to get back to my truest passion: helping organizations implement sustainable improvements and thrive.

Some years later, I was at the Amsterdam airport following a client project, waiting to fly back to the U.S. Imagine my surprise when I heard someone behind me call my name. Turning around, I saw Fred with his wife, Aura, waiting for the same return flight. After catching up, we talked about the viral success of his book, and the challenge he faced regarding requests to implement the insights from his book. Knowing that my expertise centered on implementing improvement initiatives, Fred proposed that we co-author a book to help "connect the dots between knowing and doing." After a couple of years of juggling overloaded schedules and planning, we were finally preparing to write the first draft when Fred tragically fell ill and passed away.

This finished product contains the best insights from those many hours of discussions combined with more than three decades of my insights from leading successful team-transformation initiatives. And not just at Disney, but also at numerous other world-class organizations—so you get the very best (and next) practices for your *team's* benefit. The book showcases the tools that dozens of the best companies in numerous industries, including healthcare, use to ensure that team leaders like you can make it as easy as possible to achieve consistent excellence.

What in the World Can Disney (And Other Leading Companies) Teach Me About Healthcare?

When most people think of Disney, they think only of Mickey Mouse, pixie dust, magic castles, and kiddie rides. Obviously, fantasy is no way to run a hospital—or any legitimate business, for that matter. What possible value could business tips from Disney and other renowned organizations provide a healthcare organization like yours?

As someone who spent more than 25 years running a wide variety of Disney operations, I have a behind-the-scenes insight for you: Disney's business isn't successful because of pixie dust. People think about fluffy fantasy when they think of Disney because that is exactly what the Disney organization wants you to think. It's good for their business! Disney spends millions (and millions) of dollars on marketing to influence you to focus on their fantasy world. Like any world-class organization, they want to distract you from the real-life, mundane operational things that don't add value to your experience, so you see only the extraordinary aspects that make you want to rave about them.

This book is *not* about Disney fantasy; it is about how to consistently create amazing operational results.

In the very real world.

It's about how you can thrive in a volatile, uncertain, and complex healthcare environment, by using proven tools that can make it easier for you and your team to overcome the chaos and provide the care you've always wanted to. I'll include some relevant Disney examples, but most of this book centers on other world-class companies and healthcare organizations that my team and I have worked with over the years, such as (name drop alert!) Mayo Clinic, Cleveland Clinic, Johnson & Johnson, Google, Marriott, and Apple. They all use operational insights that can dramatically help you and your healthcare team.

Disney and these other legendary companies haven't been successful for so many decades by chance. They are committed to applying strategies and operational tools that work in the real world, and do it well enough that they look like they are just "whistling while they work." They design every aspect of their operations to align and work seamlessly together for optimal results. This is exactly what has positioned them to earn extraordinary loyalty and business valuation, and to continue to thrive regardless of external circumstances (such as a pandemic). Like Disney, other world-class organizations in various industries follow the same path, with similar superior results. Simply said, Disney's business success is the same as that of every other world-class organization. What works, works—regardless of where it is implemented.

Make no mistake: No organization is perfect, but when they effectively apply their proven "team-centric" business approach, they typically dominate that industry's landscape. Implementing what works best within any situation naturally creates successful outcomes, just as it can in your healthcare arena.

The good news is that you can achieve these same extraordinary results in your healthcare organization using those strategies and tactical tools. This book spotlights the connection between healthcare and other leading organizations, the big-picture approach to successful change, and, most important, the step-by-step implementation path to get you to your goals.

Why Me? From Mouse Ears to Transforming Healthcare

I'm an accidental transformation expert. I didn't so much write the insights and implementation tools in this book as discover them.

I grew up surrounded by heroes. My family is chock full of military, first responders, and healthcare professionals. Serving, protecting, and caring for those in need is just how we rolled. Being dedicated to doing things well (smart and efficiently) was simply the right thing to do. In fact, anything that prevents that, such as foolish issues that create unnecessary work, well ... it ticks me off. I take it personally.

In fact, some of my earliest memories are of watching medical dramas on TV with my nurse turned hospital executive mother constantly ranting at the screen that "*they aren't following proper protocol!*", so it made total sense that my plan was to go into healthcare—right after a quick summer job at Disney to earn some of my tuition, which stunned my family and friends. You see, I'm not at all a theme-park guy. I'm much more of a national-parks guy; I prefer real-life nature and "more important things" in life. But once I got firsthand experience with the way Disney operated behind the scenes, I must admit I was impressed. The onstage fantasy world of characters, parades, and rides was supported backstage by a remarkably sophisticated, real-world-focused operation, with hundreds of different jobs to explore.

Suddenly, I was in the world's premier business playground—and I was hooked.

Over the next 26 years and numerous promotions, countless frustrating ordeals flared up. Each time, I knew that these situations could be better, but I wasn't sure how. So I did what came naturally: I jumped into the fray and fought my way through it. As a hyper-pragmatic operations guy, I identify with my two favorite Walt Disney quotes: "It's kind of fun to do the impossible," and "The way to get started is to quit talking and begin doing."

Leading teams from just three to more than 1,400, I encountered adversities from reinvigorating the zombie-like to unifying those on the verge of a physical death match—all with seemingly impossible production goals. Thanks to operational necessity and demanding mentors, I became a battle-scarred but skilled leader who was trusted to take on Disney's toughest organizational initiatives, including the massive challenge of spearheading the company-wide transformation effort that eventually sparked the famed "Disney Decade" of astronomical growth in the '90s—which was founded on strategies and tactical tools they still use today. These are the same strategies and tools that I helped create and implement across all levels of the corporation.

The same strategies and implementation tools I'm sharing with you now.

Since retiring from Disney, I've been fortunate to work with more great leaders across dozens of Fortune 500 companies and healthcare organizations, and have learned two remarkable facts:

1. The greatest companies follow the same path to sustainable world-class excellence.
2. The key to organizational success is the people who actually implement—specifically, effective teams at every level.

Generally, most people are doing the best they *think* they can. Unfortunately, they are often wrong. With some strategic shifts in what you do and how you do it, you can make a life-changing difference that matters most.

Achieving consistent, fantastic results doesn't have to be so hard. I hate seeing people suffer because they don't know how these legendary companies, who make it look so easy, actually make it happen. Being at the top of your industry is never easy, but it *is* doable—*if* you have the right approach. I'm eager to share those secrets with you and my extended healthcare family!

I still get irate when things aren't the way they should be, because everyone suffers—leaders, staff, patients, *everyone*. Although I can't fix all the world's problems by myself, I can make a bigger difference by helping you to make your healthcare business right. If we all simply make our part of the world better, everything will get easier and better.

One final thing about me: I love seeing teams like yours finally achieve the breakthrough you've always wanted. I've experienced firsthand how my family and friends in healthcare have struggled unnecessarily, and this is totally unacceptable—and preventable! My "why" is to protect and serve you and help you face the threatening "dragons" of your world—to make it a better place for everyone on your team and the patients you care for.

Because it matters.

Because it desperately needs to (finally) get done.

Because, together, we *can* do this.

You just need to start.

> *"Because the people who are crazy enough to believe they can change the world are the ones who actually do."*
>
> **— Iconic 1997 Apple commercial**

SELF-EXAM: WHAT ARE YOUR TEAM VITALS?

- How satisfied are you with your team's current way of working together?
- Do you sense that your team could be more productive than it is?
- Are you dissatisfied enough to begin actively working toward improvements?

Why You? From Frustration to the Outcomes of Your Dreams

When I work with professionals in struggling organizations, they invariably talk about how complicated their business is, how different it is from other businesses or industries, and how exasperated they are by being swamped with a never-ending list of tasks every day—and they seem to be on the verge of resigning themselves to this status quo.

The truth is, there is no business *exactly* like yours. Anywhere. As you know, even hospitals in the same market can be dramatically different—despite facing the same local community dynamics, workforce, and economics. Using the lack of sameness to not look for existing solutions is an excuse made by those who have given up or don't know the options already working across many real-world organizations. In both healthcare and, yes, even nonclinical organizations.

The fact that consistent excellence is happening elsewhere proves it can be achieved. Optimizing your potential does not require an excessive amount of time or resources. You don't need to overhaul your entire organization to make things better. The tools in this book are intended to guide you and your team through the transformation you deserve—without having to wait for other departments or divisions to begin. With focused effort on proven low- or no-cost tools from the most successful operations in the world, you can accomplish your goals much more easily than you'd expect. Success is all about engaging people—the very people you want to make a difference with.

You are part of a different breed; healthcare requires a very peculiar passion to help people. In fact, I see it as more than a profession. I think you were drawn to healthcare as part of a deeper calling.

One thing is for sure: You didn't get into healthcare to be chronically frustrated or burned out. But continuing to function the way that you and your team have will take a toll. You still want to make a difference—so take back your calling! Just a handful of improvements can make it easier to get better outcomes and much higher fulfillment in your clinical profession. These pages provide guidance to bridge the gap between where you and your team are and where you want to be. The world-class approach to optimizing team performance outlined in this book has been proven to work under the most difficult conditions (yes, even healthcare!), for any type of team—and it's loaded with ideas that you and your team can digest in a few hours and chew on for years.

Obviously, you are ready for a long-overdue breakthrough! The question to focus on now is: How?

And no, the answer isn't (freaking) "pixie dust." You need behind-the-scenes solutions that are the most relevant to your day-to-day team operations. Which is why I spent years making sure this book contains all the most practical implementation tools to make it easier for you to provide the healthcare excellence you started your career in healthcare to achieve.

IMPORTANT RESOURCE:

*I've created worksheets for all the tools in this book, which you can download for free at **ResultsStat.com/BookResources**. You'll also find other resources there to help you succeed in your implementation efforts.*

That said, every team's and organization's circumstances are different—and evolve over time. It is important that you explore the insights and tools in this book through *your* unique perspective and adapt (rather than just adopt) whatever specific tips are most relevant to your situation. I encourage you to refer back to the book as you move along your improvement journey, testing and adjusting different ideas as you go. Engage others in these topics and use them to spark discussions, with a bias for action.

Despite the profoundly challenging circumstances you may be in, I intend this collection of solutions to be, first and foremost, a resource of hope. No matter what ridiculousness is happening around you, you and your team can still make the difference you've always wanted. I'm confident that implementing these proven strategies and tools will lead you, step-by-step, to your very own world-class healthcare-team results—*stat*!

"We would accomplish many more things if we did not think of them as impossible."

– Vince Lombardi

For your *free* workbook download, in a larger, more user-friendly format, just visit **ResultsStat.com/BookResources** or use this QR code for your convenience:

EXTRA BONUS RESOURCE

For those executives who are planning an organization-wide change initiative, this book is written to address the foundational team improvements that collectively provide the momentum for an entire organization to improve. Your role, as an executive in your healthcare organization, is to orchestrate these team improvements in alignment with an overarching shift involving how you select new hires, how you onboard and train them, and how you engage and communicate across your workforce, as well as to reinforce effective behaviors to achieve a culture of consistent and sustainable excellence. That is a separate, distinct process that I would be honored to help you with - but until then, you can access my free downloadable road map to support your planning at **ResultsStat.com/TransformationRoadMap**.

(I bet your leadership would benefit from this resource, so feel free to share the link—and this book—with them!)

SECTION TWO

Prepare Yourself

2

Leading Change for Your Healthcare Team

So, how are you and your team doing with all the changes? Confused? Frustrated? Overwhelmed?

Consider yourselves human (and "normal").

The healthcare landscape has grown more volatile and ambiguous over the years. Increasing consumer expectations, escalating costs, aging demographics, and economic concerns are clashing with a tsunami of new technologies (to include cyber-attacks—ugh!) and innovations—all of which are impacting your patients and your team. Healthcare professionals like you are urgently looking for a solution to stop the madness and establish a secure place for the clinical care you chose to dedicate your life to.

U.S. Surgeon General Vivek H. Murthy stated in his 2022 *Advisory on Building a Thriving Health Workforce,* "As we transition towards recovery, we have a moral obligation to address the long-standing crisis of burnout, exhaustion, and moral distress across the health community. We owe health workers far more than our gratitude. We owe them an urgent debt of action."[1]

The National Institute for Occupational Safety and Health cites the following stressors specific to healthcare professionals:[2]

---

[1] Murthy, 2022, 4.

[2] NIOSH, 2018.

- Intensely stressful and emotional situations in caring for those who are sick
- Exposure to human suffering and death
- Unique pressures from relationships with the patients, family members, and employers
- Working conditions with ongoing risk for hazardous exposures to contagious diseases, hazardous medications
- Demanding physical work and risk of injuries such as from patient handling
- Long and often unpredictably scheduled hours of work related to as-needed scheduling, unexpected double shifts, and unpredictable intensity of on-call work
- For many health workers, unstable and unpredictable work lives, and financial strain
- High administrative burdens and little control over schedules

According to a recent report in the *Journal of General Internal Medicine*, physicians, nurses, clinical staff, and nonclinical support workers in healthcare are experiencing substantial levels of frustration and burnout from our collective approach to healthcare. The percentage reporting burnout was very similar among nurses (56 percent), clinical staff (54 percent), doctors (47 percent), and nonclinical staff (46 percent). Lead researcher Dr. Lisa Rotenstein, an assistant professor of medicine at Harvard Medical School, writes, "Every member of the healthcare team is really critical to patient outcomes and patient experiences of care ... It's just really important for us to remember that as we are trying to optimize both patient outcomes and experiences for our workforce."[3]

I could include whole chapters of other studies that detail the obvious conclusion that everyone agrees things need to improve. Unfortunately, we can't just defibrillate the system and make everything better—but we can explore the real-world tools the best organizations use to successfully implement change.

First, we need to (briefly!) explore the bigger picture and why most

---

[3] M Rotenstein et al., 2023.

hit a roadblock in their attempt to make things better. If you're going to successfully make changes, it's vitally important to better understand change, specifically regarding the unique dynamics of your healthcare world. This context will help the enclosed tools, and everything connected to this proven process, make better sense. In other words, don't skip this section!

The "Peculiar" Healthcare Culture

Working in a hospital is full of bizarre dichotomies. You can be in a room where a parent, overcome with joy, is holding their child for the first time, then walk to another room and see a parent, overcome with grief, holding their child for the last time. It's a place where people are victims of what life has done to them, or of what they have done to themselves. Moments of grief. Moments of joy. Moments of gross. Moments of tenderness. Many moments of intensity and urgency. No doubt, the healthcare world is certainly unique in many ways.

The healthcare industry is more complicated than most (but not all), more technical than most (but not all), and more "mysterious" than most (but not all). The significant issue that separates healthcare from most other industries is that healthcare is all of these things, *and* profoundly, intimately personal. Very few other organizations have to deal with such a wide range of extreme circumstances, with "customers" who are injured or sick, and uncomfortable and scared and disoriented and overwhelmed. Not to mention the equally distressed loved ones who accompany many of them. Emotions are high in an environment they do not understand or control. In the midst of all this, we are expected to heal or cure them as soon as possible, with minimal discomfort or inconvenience. In many instances, we are required to provide these (expensive) services whether they can afford to pay or not! What other industry is under such demanding expectations? What other industry literally "saves the day" for these vulnerable people? The healthcare industry is clearly unique—and one that desperately needs to be world-class.

Yet another vital issue to consider before jumping into a change effort: Every healthcare organization is a dynamic mixture of personalities (staff and patients) interacting in a wide range of circumstances, from highly technical to highly interpersonal. It's also a mix of adrenaline-pumping, high-pressure conditions with rare opportunities to catch your breath (never say "It's slow"!)

Contrary to popular belief, improving healthcare is not about processing more patients—that is a manufacturing model. Furthermore, improving healthcare is not about simply creating a pleasant transaction—that is a service-delivery model. The experience is much more personal (even, at times, invasive!) and complex (an endless combination of clinical and psychological variables), and requires a multidimensional approach for sustainable, thriving outcomes.

The Same Kind of Different

While the healthcare industry has peculiar elements, it shares aspects with any other industry where a group of highly educated people with different skills works together to deliver a product or service to help someone who needs what you provide and is willing to compensate you sufficiently. While there will always be exceptions in both clinical and nonclinical functions, the backbone of any healthcare organization's success is optimizing how effectively its many teams interact and perform in an orchestrated way. The ability to do so adds value to those they serve, through utilizing team resources most efficiently. This is at the heart of every organization that has achieved consistent and sustainable success. This doesn't make these organizations perfect. It simply makes them different, better, and worthy of the success they earn.

> Your situation is unlike any other! (However...)

For this reason, renowned organizations make a point to "discover" best practices from wherever they can glean them—then adapt them to their own circumstances. Notice that I didn't say they "adopt" the ideas from other companies. The key is to adjust any idea you get from any domain in a way that provides value to those you serve (patients, clients, customers), your colleagues, and your business operations. More often than not, the best breakthrough ideas have come from sources that are *not* related to your industry at all.

We've all seen it: Suddenly, a business is doing something in a totally different way that wows the customers in that target market. The business gains market share, and the competition scrambles to copy the new idea. A transformational idea is a game changer because no one else in your industry is doing it. Exploring other industries with a "What would that look like in healthcare?" attitude is a fantastic way to spark creative ideas, which lead to innovative improvements. Rarely does a truly game-changing idea bubble up in isolation within our own industry. It's not that other industries are better, merely that they are different, which is a catalyst for thinking differently—and fertile ground for your desperately needed breakthrough.

Despite the external pressures you face in healthcare, remember that it has one thing in common with every other industry. You are part of a group of wildly different people (who are constantly changing) who must effectively manage what they do and how in order to serve other wildly different people (who are constantly changing) in an increasingly complicated and challenging environment (that is also constantly changing).

"Your life does not get better by chance; it gets better by change."

— Jim Rohn

The Healthcare Change Machine

Pandemics and other ongoing chaotic healthcare-industry gyrations aside, here's the reality:

- Change will not stop—in fact, the pace will continue to increase in speed.
- Investing effort to improve how you adapt to change will serve you for the rest of your life.
- Helping others in your organization better manage change will multiply your impact.

You must be ready to influence those changes, so they are actually the improvement your patients and colleagues need.

The question is, will you?

Yes, there are plenty of excuses and a million different circumstances that complicate your situation and make things a challenge for you. Yet, while many struggle with those same circumstances, there are other healthcare professionals like you who somehow get better results—so it *is* possible. They are, in their own imperfect way, effectively dealing with the messy circumstances in their healthcare world by focusing on what they *can* do to improve—even a little bit—whatever they can.

At the risk of sounding like some coffee-mug slogan, now is the time to focus less on what you *can't* do, and more on what you *can* do. (Just writing that sentence made me dry heave a little. This is no time for *Chicken Soup* platitudes. But for real-world solutions, focusing on what you *can* do is the better investment of your time and effort!)

Next, it's necessary to overview what world-class teams understand and what most others neglect when starting any new endeavor: how to approach the bigger picture of change so your efforts gain traction and create long-term improvements that matter. While there are important processes and other dynamics involved, by far the factor that makes or breaks any change effort is "the people factor."

Change-Initiative Autopsy

You may be wondering, "How can I successfully improve things in such a complicated environment?" Well, let's do a quick review of what *not* to do and examine why most change efforts fail, so you can avoid wasting your precious time and effort.

You've probably experienced your fair share of "change initiatives" that failed to get the results you wanted. In fact, numerous studies in *Harvard Business Review* and other publications report that up to 70 percent of organizational change initiatives fall short of expectations. Recently, researchers at Bain & Company observed that "good intent, embodied in a new strategy or the design of a new operating model, will take you only so far. To realize the full benefit, mindsets and behaviors—how people think and act every day—need to change. Buying the gym set doesn't make you fit;

the habit of exercise does. Consider the track record of change programs in the corporate world. Only 12% of companies actually achieve what they set out to accomplish. Some 38% fail by a wide margin, capturing less than half of the value they initially targeted. And 50% settle for a significant dilution of results. The disturbing implication: Over time, too many organizations unwittingly wind up accepting mediocre performance."[4]

It's understandable. People are complicated (both inside and outside your organization). Organizations are full of people. Change isn't easy, so people resist.

So, given all this, what works best? Let's start with the common mistakes you should *not* do.

Based on dozens of organizational change initiatives I've led over the years, here's why change efforts—both organizational and team—often fall painfully short of their goals:

- They are overly complicated. (*Too complex* means *not implemented.*)
- They aren't in clear alignment with your organization's core mission or values, which ultimately unifies the organization. (So there's no support.)
- They measure the wrong things, which either are irrelevant or aim too low. These things may look good in a report, but they don't translate to a real-world sense of improvement (and they certainly don't create a patient or staff experience worth advocating).
- They fail to sufficiently prepare and involve those who need to implement the plan. (No involvement means no buy-in, ownership, or passion.)
- They fail to take the actions necessary to actually improve the issues identified by patients and/or staff. Fear of failure causes failure to launch, which causes a vicious cycle of repeated failure and fear and frustration. (Does this sound familiar?)

Of course, there are numerous "in between" issues that connect all these causes together, but the end result is massive chaos: disappointment,

---

[4] Bird et al., 2016.

wasted effort, wasted resources, and frustration.

Let's put an end to this nonsense!

Overcoming Frustration Overload

Personally, there's nothing more frustrating to me than working hard only to discover that something is undermining my efforts. Most healthcare professionals I know don't mind working hard if they make progress toward their passion: to make a real difference in the lives of people who need them most. One of the most common causes of failure in change attempts is miscalculating key aspects of the whole "getting people to adapt to doing new things" dilemma. Understanding the bigger picture, from the dynamics of change to the dynamics of your workplace, will help you successfully influence and navigate the process. So, to start, let's step back to consider some more insights about change that most healthcare professionals don't take the time to think about.

If you are stressed out from being tossed around by the volatile, convulsively changing healthcare environment and are looking for solutions, consider these points:

- You don't control the insanity of the healthcare environment—so trying to anticipate what regulations or patient expectations will be five years from now is futile.
- Current federal regulations are a knee-jerk reaction to the public outcry about the subpar experience they have during healthcare treatment.
- Current organizational structures in most healthcare facilities are built on standardizing processes and finding efficiencies, neither of which tends to be agile or easily adaptive to massive environmental pressures to change.
- Constant change in a corporate culture that is poorly suited to adapt is causing medical errors, damaging morale and engagement, and feeding staff burnout.

I'm not pointing these out to make you feel more stressed. I'm just pointing out the fact that you don't (and can't) control the big-picture challenges of the healthcare industry. More important, you shouldn't try to control them.

This book is all about you and your team, and how you can achieve your very best outcomes—regardless of all the mayhem that is swirling outside your healthcare doors. You can simply focus on influencing your *team's* improvement—something that is far more realistic and possible. (Of course, once you've successfully accomplished that, you will be in a much better position to influence farther-reaching improvements in other parts of your organization—but that's a whole other discussion).

> Those who resist change fall in the "do nothing" category—and wonder why things get worse.

For your own peace of mind, and the well-being of your colleagues and patients, block those bigger forces out and start investing your limited energy in things you can absolutely influence. Turn your attention to the aspects of your calling that you can personally connect with. Who is directly influenced by what you do daily? And who is affected by those you influence?

Remind yourself and your colleagues of what you do and do not have control over. Then devote yourself fully to what matters most: You and your team's mission of caring for patients who desperately need you!

"Fixing is the antidote for frustration."

– Mark David Jones

So, What Can You Do?

The transformation of an industry, or a healthcare system, or a hospital or a clinic does not succeed because of mere policy or process changes. Lasting improvements come when people—like those on your team—change their behaviors. Amid all this chaos, you can choose to respond in two ways:

1. Do nothing different—and continue to struggle and fall further behind until you become obsolete.
2. Make changes to optimize you and your team's potential.

(By the way, those who consistently resist change by claiming "that will never work here, because our situation is different" always fall into the "do nothing" category—and wonder why circumstances keep getting worse.) Embracing the *right* change results in improvement. The right improvements result in better outcomes. Better outcomes result in more than enough satisfaction to go around.

To effectively navigate this new approach, it will help to better understand how healthcare's unique dynamics affect the process of implementing sustainable improvements.

The Fundamentals of Change: What to Expect

Here are key things to keep in mind while making the effort to lead change:

- Improvements happen to fill a need.
- Improvements don't happen without someone leading the effort.
- Change, whether team, organizational, or social, happens one person at a time.
- Having a proven road map for successful change optimizes efficiency (and reduces frustrations).
- Even under the best circumstances, change is not perfectly linear, mostly because of the somewhat unpredictable but constant variable known as "people."
- The best way to improve the organization around you is to improve your team.
- The best way to improve your team is to improve you.
- Don't force revolutionary change on a regular basis. Instead, emphasize consistent, incremental improvements that are more reasonable (and tolerable) to the team.
- Helping your team improve can benefit the larger organization

and the careers of everyone on your team (and fulfill your personal calling!)

That said, one of the first things we need to understand to successfully navigate change is how the process naturally occurs and, specifically, what we can do to optimize the outcome. Probably the most common approach taken by the best organizations I've worked with is the Prosci (combining the words *professional* and *science*) ADKAR Model, which characterizes the process for individual change in five steps:[5]

- **A**wareness of the need to change (to what extent are the current circumstances unacceptable?)
- **D**esire to participate in and support the change (is the improvement worth my time and effort?)
- **K**nowledge about how to change (do I understand the process of changing?)
- **A**bility to implement new skills and behaviors (do I have the training required to successfully participate in the process?)
- **R**einforcement to keep the change in place (how will we support making the improvement "stick"?)

Essentially, these five steps reflect the natural progression of how people engage in any significant change effort. Every person on your team will go through each phase at a different pace, but all are eventually needed to fully manage, implement, and sustain the improvement effort. Each one of these steps requires different tools to be successful, and we will cover them in more detail in the upcoming implementation chapters. For now, keep this bigger picture in the back of your mind as we continue introducing the more vital dynamics surrounding the improvements you want to make with your healthcare team.

Not Just Change

When you ask people to change, they will often push back. We've all seen it. Decades of research indicate that this is a natural human response.

[5] Hiatt, 2006.

Ironically, if you ask those same people if they would like to improve (rather than change) things, most will say yes—despite the fact that, logically, it is impossible to improve anything without changing it.

This change-versus-improvement difference is not just lame wordplay. Humans resist change because most of us have been burned by change in the past. We've all been asked to make changes that, for whatever reason, weren't what we considered an improvement.

So, what is really getting in the way?

Ultimately, having been burned by change is the cause of most resistance to change. While many assume that faulty processes or limited resources are to blame for aborted change efforts, the strongest influence by far is human nature: fear of the unknown, fear of failure, fear of accountability, even the fear of change itself (metathesiophobia). Some people are even afraid of the word *fear*, so they substitute it with the word *concern*. Whatever you (or those you work with) call it, it's getting in your way—causing you and those you serve unnecessary pain and suffering. Let's get at how to resolve this common barrier.

As humans, our path to fear starts with worry, or mentally dwelling on a problem. If we feed that concern, it grows to anxiety, or feeling uneasy about an issue you can't control. If we allow that to develop, it eventually leads to fear of the perceived threat.

In the movie *After Earth*, Will Smith's character shares an insight about fear while preparing his son to begin a dangerous journey:

> Fear is not real. The only place that fear can exist is in our thoughts of the future. It is a product of our imagination, causing us to fear things that do not at present and may not ever exist. That is near insanity. Do not misunderstand me, danger is very real, but fear is a choice. We are all telling ourselves a story.

No matter where we are in the process, these unhealthy emotional barriers to growth are always attached to a scary future that may never happen.

New policies or procedures will not resolve fear. Fear is an emotional challenge that requires a *relational* solution. This is what trips up most teams trying to navigate any improvement effort. Building trust and credibility takes time and typically isn't taught in college medical classes. Thankfully, any learned bad habit (such as fear) can be unlearned.

People are complicated. People in complicated circumstances are even more complicated. The best weapon we have against fear is to know more about ourselves and understand the nature of pushing through discomfort. Helping your team identify their concerns and then bridge the gap between where they are and where they need to be will propel you past the biggest stumbling block of any change initiative. The vast majority of teams I've worked with over the years have identified that addressing the *emotional* aspect of resisting change was the key to achieving breakthroughs.

> Addressing the emotional aspect of resisting change is the key to achieving breakthroughs

Metathesiophobia and Your Team

Fear isn't magically cured by superior logic. Fear is overcome by relational issues such as building trust, credibility, and the confidence to act despite that fear.

That said, no, you can't just yoga your way into a better team situation.

Don't get me wrong, there are many different approaches to managing fear, but I'm not going to get into specific adaptation techniques, like controlled breathing and journaling. These are popular intrapersonal activities that can help to some degree (go with whatever works for you personally), but the focus here will be more related to practical workplace steps that overcome problematic fear or concern.

The best way to manage being overwhelmed and fearful is to resolve the root causes of those issues. The stress that you and your team feel is intensified by the frustration of you falling short of your healthcare potential. Improve those circumstances and you'll improve the outcomes—and improve your stress levels!

So, let's get to it!

There are three primary considerations regarding fear when initiating any change effort:

1. Face it: One surefire way to help people push through fear is to have them value the goal on the other side of that fear more ("I'm afraid of water, but I will swim across the canal if my child is in danger on the other side"). A vested interest in the outcome that is stronger than the obstacle you are concerned about fuels your motivation to overcome that fear. Quickly.
2. Understand it: Fear is more powerful when it is mysterious. To combat this problem, start learning more about the circumstances that cause your emotional reaction and inhibit your progress. Chances are, the more you understand the actual situation (rather than the assumed or perceived one), the more you will realize that it doesn't deserve your fear. This knowledge reveals insights about the most effective ways to work through the problem.
3. Overcome it: Once you've figured out the cause of the fear, conquer the actual obstacle in your way. A key aspect of this step is reinforcing support to ensure that the problem is no longer a threat to future efforts. Gaining knowledge and skill leads to earned confidence—which is the very best fear buster I know of!

"Courage is just fear that holds out a little longer."

– General Douglas MacArthur

Finally, involve everyone affected by the change. Identifying their ultimate goal (such as providing a better patient experience and making a difference to those they care for), then ensuring that they have significant influence over the details of the change, will help tremendously—especially once they see that empowerment in action. Your ability to deliver on these obstacles to change will make the difference between a successful transformation and another frustrating "program of the month" disappointment.

Approaching change from the perspective of those you serve (and who serve your patients) can provide the breakthrough you need to thrive in any change event.

Fear that is not effectively managed, multiplies. Multiplied fear creates confusion—and more fear. And more confusion.

> **SELF-EXAM**
>
> Consider something you used to be afraid of. What specifically changed? Likely, time and experience; you gradually got more comfortable with the issue. This is clinically referred to as "systematic desensitization," and done in the right way, it can work wonders. How can that solution be applied to your situation?

You and every person on your team are driven by different deep-seated concerns. Your responsibility, if you want to influence your team's effort, is to help identify them and engage your team to help them improve the issues. It's been said that "fear is a bully—once confronted, it retreats." Table 2-1 contains actions to consider while going through this process yourself, before approaching others on your team to do so.

Table 2-1. Getting Yourself Through Fear

Actions	Tactics	Self-Exam
Face It	▪ Invest uninterrupted time to solve. ▪ Arrange trusted support for accountability.	▪ What fears or concerns hold you back? ▪ What compelling goal is on the other side of resolving this fear? ▪ Commit to taking action with trusted colleagues.
Understand It	▪ Reflect on the source of the fear. ▪ Identify the associated emotions. ▪ Learn more about the issue.	▪ When did the fear begin? What makes it worse? ▪ What affects the circumstances that trigger fear? ▪ What emotions are appropriate or most effective?
Overcome It	▪ Plan systematic desensitization (gradually increasing interaction). ▪ Develop skills that overcome. ▪ Document progress.	▪ Spend more time "near" the circumstances that spark the fear—more and more often. ▪ What excuses have you relied on in the past? ▪ Note what makes it easier or harder and improve

Beginning the process of removing barriers of fear for yourself is a vital first step, but eventually, you will need to engage your team to work through the improvement effort. We'll delve into this more deeply (with more tools, of course) when we get to Chapter 6, on teams. What fears might those you interact with face? Your patients and/or their families? Your colleagues? Your boss? What is at risk from their perception? What are their high-pressure concerns? What can you do or say to help alleviate them? Consider the following questions in advance (Table 2-2):

Table 2-2. Understanding the Fears of Others

I Care For	Possible Fears or Concerns	Root Cause: Why?	What "Change Help" They Need
Patients			
Colleagues			
Boss			
Other			

Starting with our problem (fear), we can connect the dots between that issue and the things that resolve it. What kills fear (usually of the unknown)? Legitimate confidence (not feigned bravado). True confidence comes from being capable. Capability comes from consistently effective practice and preparation. The most effective preparation starts with becoming more aware of your perceptions of the fear itself.

Let's look at proven action steps for developing the right perception, right preparation, and right capability.

Action Steps for Fighting Fear

Action Step One: Right Perception

The first step in fighting fear is to achieve a realistic perspective. How much of an immediate threat is the perceived problem? How likely is the worst-case scenario? Psychologists guide people with phobias through "systematic desensitization." This means gradually interacting with what you fear to increase familiarity and understanding, which reduces the irrational fear.

PRO TIP

One effective way to combat fear in those who are more anxious during any improvement effort is to plan smaller, more tolerable "micro-changes." Twenty smaller change steps might be more easily attempted than five larger change steps, which will help that person navigate the process more confidently, rather than getting intimidated and then simply giving up before they start. Focus on adding one new behavior to an already established routine until it becomes an established part of how the team operates, then add the next small change. Gradually (and less painfully), you'll find the team evolving toward your larger goal.

Action Step Two: Right Preparation

The next step is to attend to the things you can directly control or influence to optimize your preparedness. In his book *Flow*, Mihaly Csikszentmihalyi introduces the phrase "control your controllables." He is referencing how, in the midst of change and instability, we gain some measure of stability (and confidence) by controlling the things we are able to effectively control. The act of resolving any controllable issues optimizes resources for any "uncontrollable" issues that remain.

Action Step Three: Right Capability

The third step for combating fear is to start developing a team culture of capable confidence. This involves three aspects:

1. Focus on others. If the stress is coming from a perceived personal shortcoming, then it is likely driven by being too focused on self. The solution is to shift focus to those you are serving—either patients and their families, or colleagues on your team.
2. Build trust. Distrust generates significant negative emotions, including fear. To resolve this situation, take action to develop trust in and from others. Often, the root of fear and trust issues is a lack of trust in self.
3. Emphasize strengths, but develop (or prevent the need for) any existing weaknesses. The more you can develop your skills and knowledge, the more capable you will be to respond effectively to challenging circumstances. Ideally, you'll aim to become so capable that the fearful scenarios are no longer perceived as a threat—and you can then comfortably perform at your highest level, even amid adversity.

Working with your team to face the unknown with the right preparation and renewed capability will lead to a culture of confidence and extraordinary outcomes. Overcoming the "fear factor" in your practice may seem intimidating, but with these insights, tools, and action steps, you can create a confident care experience that encourages staff and patients to move from being your internal and external customers to being your loyal advocates.

PRO TIP

Be aware, every new beginning requires an ending. Get clear about exactly what each member of your team must let go of to fully embrace the new direction. Some who stand to lose something important to them because of the change may resist and even sabotage the effort. You'll need to help them adjust so as not to drag down the rest of the team's progress.

The truth is, sometimes the fear doesn't go away—and we have to do it (scared) anyway. That's okay. Growth comes from that too. And then you can help someone else who is scared work through it themselves.

The Bottom Line for Change in Healthcare

Those we serve, patients and staff alike, know that things should and can be better in their healthcare experience. They have more access to information and more choices than ever before. And with better options, whether with telehealth or in-person care, it has become easier than ever to switch rather than settle for subpar interpersonal or clinical care. Michael J. Dowling, president and CEO of the award-winning Northwell Health, recently stated it well: "Over the past five or six years, we've seen major changes in the way innovative organizations in all industries treat their customers. For far too long in our industry, there was a pervasive attitude of, 'We're hospitals, or we're physicians, people will always come because we're here in the community,' but those days are over. Consumers don't want to be told when to come or what to do—they want to access care and services on their terms, not ours. We are in the consumer service business, and our patients are educated and knowledgeable. They value easy access, a pleasant experience and quality care, so it's our job to adapt quickly to meet their needs and expectations."[6]

[6] Dowling, 2017.

While many people feel that aspects of the larger healthcare universe are unhealthy and desperately need change, there is hope. There are things you can affect, and immediately: the day-to-day operations within you and your team's reach. Your team can significantly improve the care that you deliver each day using proven strategies and tactical tools from world-class organizations. Your team can create the kind of meaningful, personal care that you got into healthcare to be a part of. Yes, if every team in your organization were to do the same, it would massively transform every aspect of your community—but for now, you can choose what you can directly influence this minute: Your team.

PRO TIP

When preparing to articulate a compelling reason for your team to support the improvement effort, ponder how to best answer the following questions, which they will certainly have:

1. What will be different and better? (They need to know if the benefit—and risk—of supporting this will be worth it.)
2. Are you committed to supporting me on this unknown path? (They need to know they can count on you.)
3. How will this initiative be more successful than previous efforts that have fallen short? (They need to know that you have learned a better way since then.)

   If you can't share convincing answers to these fair questions, you aren't ready to lead this improvement attempt.

BONUS PRO TIP

Test out your answers with some trusted colleagues to discover any confusion or disagreements.

3

Building a Strategic Approach to Sustainable Success

Have you ever wondered how the same best-in-class companies stay at the top of their industry year after year? Even when an entire industry is struggling with the same circumstances of ever-higher customer expectations, shifting social trends, and tight labor pools and other resources, there is always a group of organizations that manage to thrive. Are you curious about how they do it?

Consider other healthcare organizations in your area that provide similar services. They all deal with the same external circumstances as your organization, and yet, some get better results. How is that? Even if you are getting the best results in your community, you know in your gut that you and your team (and your entire organization) can do better.

As someone who's worked directly with many of these perennial success stories, I can tell you it's not some magic wand. They have the same general resources you have. For the most part, it's not what they have that makes the difference; it's how they *use* what they have.

If the vast majority of world-class organizations in various industries practice the same approach to achieving extraordinary results for sustained success, that should get your attention—and spark you to seriously consider how you can practically adapt these best practices to your own team.

SELF-EXAM

Do you work with anyone who has a "if it wasn't invented here, it's not relevant" attitude? If so, how is that affecting your team? Learning about other successful approaches doesn't require you to outright *adopt* them—but it does provide a clue as to what works and why. And you can focus on *adapting* an approach to align with your unique circumstances. Give it a try!

While the specific nature of any service organization (yes, including healthcare) can be wildly different, the common denominator for all organizations, regardless of industry, is that they are a collection of human beings working together to serve other human beings. The details of what is done may differ, but *how* humans work effectively together remains the same. If you truly care about your outcomes, you will be open to tools for effectively working with and serving other humans—no matter the source of those breakthrough insights.

The elusive "secrets" of these world-class companies are effective—not only at the organizational level but, more important, at your team level as well. To properly implement the tools, it's vital to understand the bigger picture, so you know what to align to.

"Shallow people believe in luck and circumstance. Strong people believe in cause and effect."

— Ralph Waldo Emerson

The Proven Approach to Sustainable, Long-Term Success—That Anyone Can Do

When people talk with me about Disney, they often gush about how incredible the experience is there. Because it's consistently better than other service experiences, they tend to put it in some weird category of make-believe fluffy rainbows, unicorns, and fantasy—but you don't develop a reputation for world-class excellence by magic.

The problem with making everything look easy is that onlookers start to believe that it *is* easy. Walt Disney himself said, "People often ask me if I know the secret of success and if I could tell others how to make their dreams come true. My answer is, you do it by working."

Make no mistake—achieving excellence requires work. You have to earn it by focusing the right effort on the right things at the right time in the right way. Execution, effective and not, determines the consequences.

When it comes to healthcare operations and world-class organizations, there is good news and bad news. The bad news is that there is no such thing as "pixie dust." The good news is that I've been behind the scenes at numerous renowned organizations, and can say that you likely already have what you need to achieve extraordinary results for relatively low cost in your real world.

Appropriately identifying priorities and then mastering the discipline to consistently make progress every day (issues that are not sexy or magical in *any* way) is the only thing that leads to sustainable success, in any aspect of life. World-class organizations find a way to consistently implement their strategic priorities every single day, by implementing simple steps that every person on the team can do in strategic alignment with the overarching values and mission. Your organization can do this too, if you simply have the insights and tools, which are in the following chapters.

What Exactly Is a World-Class "Wow" Experience—And Why Do I Want One at My Healthcare Organization?

To connect the dots between your healthcare operation and world-class organizations, let's start with a brief story that captures the essence of what Disney and other dominant companies do differently and better to create consistent—and, literally, remarkable—success.

One day, our administrative offices received a three-page typed letter from a guest who went into great detail about his family's recent experience. The letter started off: "To Whom It May Concern, My family of six come to Disney World three times a year and stay for a week each time in one of your resort hotels."

This immediately got my attention. First of all, I'm thinking, "What kind of oddball wants to come to Disney three times every year?" Secondly, I'm thinking, "This family is spending a lot of money (Disney ain't cheap!), so they must be *rich* oddballs." The stakes had been raised. The next part of his opening sentence is burned into my memory: "and I've never felt compelled to write a letter until now." At this point, I knew what followed was going to be a significant issue—so I held my breath as I continued reading, thinking, "Please be a good experience! Please be a good experience!"

The letter went into great detail about how this young family has four small children. Upon arrival, they all wanted to rush out to the theme park, so off they went. While there, each kid wanted a stuffed plush toy, so they each got a different Disney character. They went back to the hotel room that night and went to sleep. The next morning, they got up to rush off to the park again. When they returned to the hotel room, they saw that all the toys were gathered in a semicircle on a bed, facing the TV, which was on the Disney Channel.

Now, let's analyze this for a minute. What do kids think happens to toys when they leave the room? They think toys come to life, right? Just like *Toy Story*! Well, the dad explains that his kids ... lost ... their ... minds, thinking they had "caught" the toys being "alive."

Well, the story doesn't end there. They eventually settled down and went to sleep. The next day, they went to the park, and came back to find them all sitting around the kitchen table with cookies and milk. The kids were amazed *again*. The following day, they return from the park—by this time, actively anticipating that the toys will have moved—and found them in the bathroom sink with little shower caps on their heads (my personal favorite). Finally, on the last full day, they returned to their room and found all the toys lined up in the window, "waiting for them to come back," according to the father.

I know. Touching moment, eh?

But that's not why you bought this book. And I'm not a fluffy story-time kinda guy. Let's break this down from a strategic and tactical-operations perspective so you can leverage the valuable insights from this experience and apply them to your *clinical* environment.

The Non-"Pixie Dust" Approach to Creating Operational Magic

Let's start with the obvious: The toys didn't move themselves; sorry to burst your bubble. They were moved around by the housekeeping hostess (her name was Judi). So, let's look at this from an operational angle: Ask yourself, what are the basic expectations of a hotel stay? Essentially, that everything is clean and where it's supposed to be (other, extra amenities like thread count, turndown service, and chocolates on the pillow are usually determined by price). What are the general responsibilities of a housekeeper? To clean everything and make sure everything is in its place. (By the way, they are held accountable to clean 14 rooms per shift!) Disney's standard operating procedures for housekeepers doesn't include moving toys around. Then why would this housekeeper dare to do such a thing?

Because Judi saw her job as more than the task she was hired to perform. (And this was *not* by accident.) How long did it take for her to wow this family? Maybe a couple of minutes? And the result was an experience that this family relayed to *hundreds* of people in the following months. Notice, too, that the millions of dollars Disney spent on rides, shows, and parades failed to garner a letter in all the previous years.

SELF-EXAM

Are you or your team limiting your efforts to the mere technical requirements of your job, or are you using low- and no-cost ways to more personally engage those you serve? How might you extend your clinical skills to include more compassionate, remarkable care?

Imagine if her boss had gotten this letter, taken the nonstrategic attitude that she was "wasting time," and berated her—maybe even adding an extra room to her workload because "she had extra time to 'play' on the job." What do you think the consequences would be? Do you think the housekeeper would move toys again? Do you think she would tell her colleagues about getting reprimanded? What are the chances that any of the other housekeepers would do something that exceeded expectations for other hotel guests? Do you think the story would leak out to other housekeepers at one of the other 30 hotels at Disney? What impact do you think it would have on their willingness to go beyond cleaning and organizing? When an organization prioritizes the wrong things, the customer (and employee) experience begins a downward "death spiral" that undermines virtually every facet of the operation.

SELF-EXAM

Do you see this kind of limited thinking among your team? What are examples of making shortsighted decisions that create long-term problems?

Your Outcomes are Natural Consequences

The key components of what naturally creates success hold true for organizations and teams alike. Noted business researcher Fred Reichheld conducted a groundbreaking study of what world-class businesses do differently and better to achieve consistent superior results. One of the key findings in his March–April 1993 *Harvard Business Review* article, which spawned numerous best-selling books, was an overarching strategy showing a causal relationship among several important aspects of any business operation.[7]

- **Loyalty, growth, and long-term success:** The end goal of every organization is to achieve loyalty, growth, and long-term success. Whether you work at a for-profit or not-for-profit company, you are seeking growth and mission success that will satisfy those who care most about your organization's health. You've probably heard the adage "No margin, no mission." No matter what type of healthcare organization you are, if you

[7] Reichheld, 1993.

can't afford to keep the utility bills paid, you will close—and *no* patients will get care. So, obviously, long-term success must be the goal if you want to take care of patients for the long term. The next question, then, is "What specifically causes this long-term success outcome?"

- **Extreme "customer" satisfaction:** Whether your customer is a patient, their family, or other people coming to your organization whom you help serve, the goal is not mere satisfaction, but *extreme* satisfaction. Truly engaged customers are the only people who become loyal. They will not only return when they have a choice (and they almost always have some kind of choice); they will become advocates who recommend that their family, friends, and colleagues choose your healthcare organization as well. Make no mistake, this does *not* mean that we try to act as a hotel or retail operation. However, you do have the obligation to care for them in such a way that they experience genuine compassion, respect, and dignity in their time of need. Being able to effectively care for your patients is likely the reason you got into healthcare. But this customer satisfaction doesn't just magically appear. What creates this loyalty?
- **Operational excellence:** The only way patients will be extremely satisfied is if your clinical and administrative staff delivers an experience that *consistently* exceeds their expectations. This requires a high-performing team working effectively together that insists on innovation, excellence, and efficiency for every person they care for. Continuously improving the day-to-day activities that affect the patient—and staff—experience will ultimately enhance value for the organization's stakeholders. What creates operational excellence?
- **Employee engagement:** According to Jacob Schneid of the Canadian performance-assessment firm The Momentum Group, "Engagement has been referred to as an organization's ultimate competitive advantage—and possibly the only one it can fully control."[8] When your team is fully engaged, they

are more fully committed to accomplishing any tasks that support the organization's mission and success. In contrast to most typical companies, world-class organizations view their employees as internal "customers." Supporting your colleagues as customers, and using the same tools showcased in this book to engage them, will naturally result in more committed staff—and all the benefits associated with this effort.

Interestingly, these four components align with a 2015 healthcare research study referred to as "The Quadruple Aim."[9] This observation has become popular in recent years. Essentially, the Quadruple Aim of healthcare consists of four overarching goals:

1. Improving the experience of providing care (creating meaning in work)
2. Reducing the per capita cost of healthcare
3. (Enhancing) the individual experience of care
4. Improving the health of the population (as the ultimate outcome)

Table 3-1. Comparing Loyalty Profit Chain and The Quadruple Aim

Loyalty-Profit Chain	Employee Engagement	Operational Excellence	Extreme Customer Satisfaction	Loyalty and Long-Term Success
The Quadruple Aim	Improving the experience of providing care	Reducing the per capita cost of healthcare	(Enhancing) the individual experience of care	Improving the health of the population

That said, there is one more step that was not included in Reichheld's original article (nor the later Quadruple Aim healthcare research) that is a critical consideration made by all world-class organizations. It's the response to the question "What causes the culture that develops engaged, high-performing teams?" The answer is illustrated in the following World-Class Success Chain model (Figure 3-1).

---

[8] Schneid, 2019.

[9] Sikka et al., 2015.

Figure 3-1. World-Class Success Chain Model

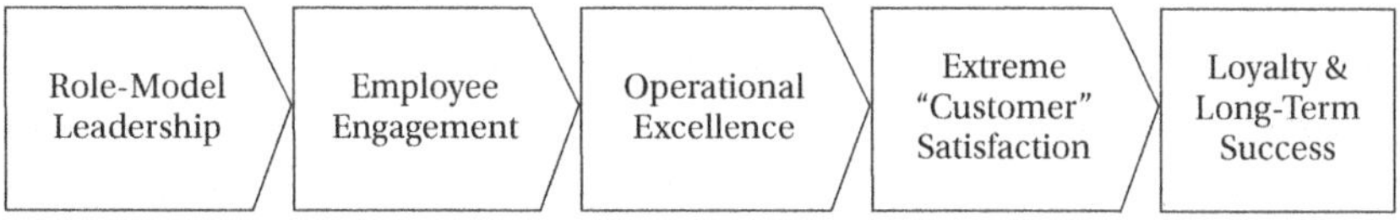

The missing aspect is what sparks the entire chain reaction: Leadership. But not merely the basic definition of *leadership* that most use. World-class organizations consider leadership differently:

Role-Model Leadership—The best companies define a leader as "anyone in the organization who has influence over the culture." This is potentially anyone employed by the organization, not just those with direct reports. When people, regardless of title, model appropriate behaviors and reinforce actions that build effective relationships and unify others toward a common goal, it opens the door to "magic"—and that can be replicated in any industry.

Role-model leaders throughout an organization are the catalysts for action, improvement, and excellence. Communicating a compelling vision, involving people across the operation, and effectively managing resources create the ideal environment within which employee engagement—and the rest of the World-Class Success Chain—can be optimized to achieve long-term, sustainable success.

"Everything Counts, All the Time"

No matter what efforts your healthcare organization is investing in marketing, the primary marketing results will always come from your patients' experiences and the stories they tell afterward.[10] (This also holds true for staff experiences and their satisfaction and loyalty.) Good or bad, word will get out to your community about all aspects of your healthcare practice: your treatment of people, your processes, your general environment. Each story either adds value or drains it. That impression of care will be compared with their expectations to determine if they are satisfied—and what they decide to do about it.

---

[10] Wolf, 2018.

In fact, according to a 2022 survey by the experience research group Qualtrics XM, based on 24,000 people in 24 countries, there is a strong correlation (0.77 coefficient, if you're a numbers person) between satisfaction rates and likelihood to trust.[11] Additionally, there is an even stronger (0.86 coefficient) correlation between satisfaction and likelihood to recommend, which is a vital component to staying in business. According to their findings specific to hospitals and medical clinics, those who rated the experience a 5 out of 5 were 2.7 times more likely to trust their healthcare provider and a whopping 3.54 times more likely to recommend the medical provider to family and friends than those who gave a 3 out of 5 rating.

There are many significant reasons we should care about the experience of our patients (and our colleagues). So, let's get clear about this whole "satisfaction" dynamic and how we can consistently achieve it.

We can see this scenario every day in any organization. Legendary organizations such as St. Jude Children's Research Hospital and Mayo Clinic have flourished because they consistently deliver *wow* experiences that are worth sharing with family, friends, and colleagues. And share we do. With the widespread use of social media, those opinions, good and bad, influence the decisions of untold numbers of people who care to read about them. And that affects your organization, your workplace, and, ultimately, your career and calling. Important stuff!

When people judge an experience with you to be great or disappointing or anything in between, they are not just comparing their experience with others in healthcare. People are comparing every experience you deliver with every other experience they have—regardless of industry—and judging whether it was worth it.

For example, when patients or their family complain about not knowing how long their wait will be, they are frustrated because they're comparing the uncertainty around the hospital wait with that of, say, a restaurant where they get a pager that notifies them when their table is ready. It's human nature to think to ourselves, "If my local family restaurant can provide a simple tool that relieves my wait-time anxiety, how come an expensive professional healthcare business doesn't?" We shouldn't be surprised if

---

[11] Temkin et al., 2022.

they deduct points from their satisfaction score.

Word-of-mouth comments always carry more weight than slick marketing campaigns. Your ability to influence their decisions is directly linked to your ability to make the experience valuable to them. Keep in mind, *they* determine their criteria for satisfaction.

Another thing to consider is that your patients will have numerous "micro-experiences" with different colleagues during their larger experience. Creating superior value once or twice is nice—but it isn't enough. If they get good service once, an average customer will consider it luck. If the same place delivers good service twice, they will assume it is just a coincidence. But once it happens three, four, or more times, most people will determine that the experience is by design. Delivering an experience *consistently* is what puts you in a different category. You'll hear statements like "They aren't like the other hospitals. They are different—and better!" The care you deliver becomes stories that people tell. Extraordinary experiences become extraordinary stories told by passionate people, who tell their family and friends. You've seen this happen—you likely have a few stories of your own! Consistently delivering a memorable experience translates to a memorable reputation, which translates to growth and more people cared for.

It's as simple—and as difficult—as that. But with the right blueprint and tools, you can lead your team to world-class results!

In fact, there has been significant research conducted about whether you've successfully provided an overall patient experience that resulted in a loyal advocate. Most healthcare organizations collect an enormous amount of feedback to make the best-informed decisions regarding their operations. Everything from safety to gaps in care.

You likely are familiar with CAHPS (Consumer Assessment of Healthcare Providers and Systems, or HCAHPS, if you are at a hospital), whose surveys are designed to capture patient experiences with healthcare services at multiple levels of the delivery system. It was developed to provide a "national standard for collecting and publicly reporting information about patients' experiences that allowed valid comparisons to be made across hospitals locally, regionally or nationally," according to the Centers for Medicare & Medicaid Services, which helps implement the surveys.[12] Interestingly, CAHPS's primary hospital-experience survey questions are mostly nonclinical, focusing on aspects of the patient experience that they consider when evaluating their level of satisfaction. Whichever tool you use to keep track of your outcomes and the impact you have on those you serve, it is in your best interest to understand the end goal for successfully treating your patients—based on your *patients'* criteria.

Behind the Scenes of World-Class Transformation

Disney, while not perfect, is revered for the consistently amazing successes the company has earned over the past century. This is the result of developing effective implementation tools that optimize outcomes. The sleepy little animation company of the 1920s has become a juggernaut of world-class brands, including multiple theme parks and resorts around the globe, Pixar, Marvel Studios, LucasFilms, ESPN, ABC-TV, National Geographic, Disney+, a cruise line with multiple award-winning ships—the list goes on. What people don't realize is that the company founded by Walt Disney more than 100 years ago has had several close calls with total failure. While some were the result of extreme risk taking, one in particular was the result of a decade of coasting—getting by on the great reputation Walt himself built.

Here's a quick explanation of the "near-death experience" in the mid-1980s that not many people are aware of. There were two hostile-takeover attempts made by corporate raiders, all because Disney had gotten sloppy and allowed itself to become undervalued. The company was still functioning okay, but we all knew it was far from our potential.

I vividly remember the frustration of nearly everyone in the company, feeling that we were working too hard, dealing with too many mistakes and missed opportunities. Our guests expected more. We knew we could deliver better. But things were just not coming together as they should.

(Do you and your team feel like that these days?)

At Disney, we struggled with this constant pressure to produce better outcomes. Internally, we were bombarded with metrics that left us

[12] CMS, 2008.

embarrassed, frustrated, and depressed. They pointed to problems such as:

- Industry instability
- Insufficient staffing
- Underutilized resources
- Poor teamwork/performance
- Missed deadlines
- Cost overruns/rising expenses
- Downward-spiraling morale
- Rising customer complaints

Sound familiar in your healthcare world?

I remember colleagues complaining that we were working incredibly hard to deliver a very good experience, but it fell below the extraordinary experience that we all knew in our bones we could deliver if the circumstances were better.

The Disney brand stood for excellent quality, delightful innovation, and fantastic service. We had all come to work at Disney to be part of that hard-earned "magic"—and to even build on that reputation. Disney hired capable people, and we all wanted to make a difference in the lives of those we served. No one wanted to go to work every day only to get results that fell short. Especially when we knew it didn't have to be that way.

By and large, our guests hadn't noticed the drop in effectiveness. Our pride in what we were doing and a flurry of last-second heroics usually covered up the backstage shortfalls. But the rare complaints had become more frequent—and the problems were growing. Cast members saw the writing on the wall: "Fix this growing mess before it gets out of control and all falls apart." Many started to lose hope.

The internal surveys and metrics indicated that we spent an inordinate amount of time, effort, and money trying to resolve problems that we often created *ourselves*, due to:

- Unclear and misaligned goals
- Competing priorities
- Overly redundant processes
- Sloppy communication

- Turf wars among different teams/divisions
- Poor time management
- Resistance to change
- Inconsistent approach to customers and employees

SELF-EXAM

List what feels familiar to your situation in healthcare. What aspects of your current operation need the most improvement?

Following the second "wake-up call" takeover attempt, Disney brought in two new leaders (Michael Eisner and Frank Wells) to help turn things around. After some initial effort to assess the challenges we faced, a bold plan was hatched to become a consistently, sustainably high-performing operation, resulting in a stunning transformation the media dubbed the "Disney Decade." That approach is still used today; although Disney has had some cultural challenges with the numerous acquisitions they've made over recent years, they are working to get back on track.

Performance Excellence: Unlocking the Business Behind the Magic

People often ask me what Disney's "secret sauce" is. I believe a significant part of Disney's success is rooted in their ability to create an approach that aligns and involves everyone in the organization to focus on the experience of those they serve *and* each other. This effort is founded on their wildly successful process called Performance Excellence. I'll share a brief overview for context, then connect this to your healthcare reality and next steps.

Essentially, as part of the transformation effort, my team and I identified the performance gaps throughout our operation, then conducted extensive benchmarking to determine the best solutions to bridge those gaps. We gathered best practices from various internal areas, as well as from leading external companies in a wide variety of industries. We were aware that this initial, quick-fix tactic of adapting current best practices wouldn't guarantee a competitive edge for an environment that was always evolving, so my entire transformation team committed to developing a long-term solution that would not be a "program of the month," but an ongoing process of continuous improvement that would serve the company for a sustainable future.

After gathering an extensive set of the best tools from other world-class sources, we discovered a common theme, which helped us create a blueprint that successfully delivered consistent excellence in all aspects of our operation. This initiative eventually became known as the Performance Excellence process—optimizing long-term potential in a self-perpetuating combination of strategies and tactics. The bulk of the effort was empowering the teams, who were closest to the day-to-day customer experience and therefore the linchpin to the system.

This overarching strategy for optimal performance involves:

- Providing a unifying set of non-negotiable standards (mission, vision, values) that serves as a "north-star" decision-making tool for every person in the organization
- Establishing a consistent perspective that both customers and employees are human beings and the focus of our products and services—our reason for being
- Creating operational tools that distill complicated business issues into manageable support systems that anyone can use in tandem with their functional obligations
- Fostering an ongoing expectation of engagement to involve the best insights of our employees and customers to influence our mutual growth and benefit
- Presenting a catalyst for innovation, both large and small, to encourage fresh, relevant, and valuable ideas for improving our products, services, and experiences and provide continuous growth for the future

Performance Excellence provided a systematic tactical solution that:

- Exceeded guest expectations (their word-of-mouth comments determine the future of the organization)

- Got everyone involved, so they bought in, took ownership, and became passionate about succeeding together
- Encouraged listening to others, so we learned what matters most to those we serve—outside and inside our team
- Broke down relational barriers between functional silos, so we could become a unified force
- Shared information and suggestions to multiply the benefits of improvement
- Helped us work more effectively (as defined by the guest, employee, and operational/financial metrics)
- Emphasized being a team player that collaborated effectively
- Regularly tried new ways to deliver superior results at every position, so we could agilely adjust to inevitable future changes

SELF-EXAM

How relevant are these strategies and tactics to your clinical operation? Which aspects do you feel your team could benefit from?

Whenever you have a wide variety of functions working under the same roof (like a hospital), it becomes far more complicated to coordinate those efforts toward a common goal. The secret to Disney's Performance Excellence process is that it establishes clear, operations-wide, non-negotiable goals, then involves every team in improving what matters most in the way that makes practical sense for their unique function—all in alignment with those shared goals.

The approach outlined in this book was developed for your healthcare team, and when implemented effectively, it generates remarkable results. The more teams that incorporate this approach, the more the results multiply, and the greater the benefits to your healthcare organization and community. Organizations that coordinate all teams to unify on this approach have become legends in their industry. (The additional organization-wide roll-out details are essentially the orchestration of all the individual team efforts—which may be my next book. Until then, this is all you need for your team to thrive, so keep leading forward!)

Avoiding the "Program of the Month" Curse

Now, you've probably been through some kind of change initiative during your career. Chances are, you've endured the inevitable rollout (with the posters, T-shirts, and coffee mugs) and the temporary (and typically superficial) improvements, which eventually fade away until the next initiative is announced the following year. Sadly, this is a common curse for many organizations.

> The key is to focus your healthcare team on practical actions that reinforce what matters most.

World-class companies don't follow trendy management fads. They follow tried-and-true strategies and tactics that allow real-world people in real-world teams to consistently achieve real-world results—time and time again. It's why the best organizations have earned a reputation of excellence and remain at the top of their industry year after year. The key is to focus your healthcare team on practical actions that reinforce what matters most:

- Aligning all your efforts with your core mission, vision, and values
- "Walking the talk" with integrity as a role-model (formal or informal) leader
- Fully engaging your expanded team, who is interconnected in delivering care
- Making innovative, strategic decisions with the resources available to you
- Exceeding the expectations of those you serve with compassion and care

The thread that connects all these critical actions (and that is missing from most standard change initiatives) is engaging each member of your team, and others involved in the effort, to improve the experience. There is a direct correlation between the level of involvement and the resulting levels of buy-in, ownership, and passion. Any change effort that lacks significant buy-in eventually fails. Improve your involvement to improve your buy-in—and long-term outcomes.

Make no mistake, leading team improvements is a high-wire act—especially in the volatile healthcare environment. That said, when you fully integrate these five facets of your team operations, you will be on your way to the breakthrough you desire.

No Margin, No Mission. Period.

Another thing to consider is a larger-scale perspective of what ultimately fuels your healthcare organization's operation—and your team's existence. Whether you are a for-profit or not-for-profit organization, or a functional team that bills for clinical services or one that is a support-function expense, you are responsible for providing *value* that grows your mission to care for people who need your help. The adage "No margin, no mission" is a truism. If you can't manage your resources effectively and can't finance your hospital's operational bills and get closed down, you will not be taking care of anyone.

End of story. End of mission. End of calling.

Listen, I get it—you likely didn't get into healthcare to deal with business issues, but considering money issues is a necessary concern. Your resources are all you have to serve with. Growing your resources merely allows you to positively affect even more people— and better achieve the goal of your healthcare calling. You must shift your thinking toward appropriately adding so much value to those you serve (both externally and internally) that it convinces those who fund your operation to invest more in your team.

The resources your team legitimately needs to best care for your patients must be worth the investment in the eyes of those who decide how the budget is distributed. Those decision makers are guided by the ultimate source(s) of those funds. Keeping those sources on your radar will help you communicate your value in connection with what matters most to those allocating your resources. The challenge is in how you prove your worth persuasively to them. Creating a team culture that consistently delivers results is the best way to grow your operation and enjoy a career of making the difference you always wanted to make.

This Is Relevant for Your Healthcare Team's Performance Excellence

Here are the key takeaways for you:

- This approach to sustainable improvement is the result of combining the best practices of leading organizations in numerous industries (sufficient for short-term gains), which propel into "next practices" (thought leadership that translates to improvements in all functions that adapt to the constantly changing business landscape). It is practiced by virtually every world-class organization in every industry—private or public sector.
- Although Disney rolled out this Performance Excellence initiative across the entire organization (which is likely not your situation), the primary ideas, results, and momentum were driven by the individual teams (which you *are* able to influence).
- We discovered that senior or divisional leadership support, although helpful, was not necessary for team success. In fact, in most cases, the strongest momentum came from teams who achieved visible results, then inspired other teams to begin participating. The outcomes spoke volumes, and eventually all teams and leaders eagerly committed to its implementation simply to enjoy the many benefits.

Having experienced the process of researching, developing, designing, implementing, and maintaining Performance Excellence during my career at Disney and then later, at dozens of leading organizations, my team and I have realized three important and timeless truths:

1. For long-term success, the way you achieve the results (with

integrity to your mission, vision, and values) is as important as the result itself.

2. The only practical way to be sustainably agile and relevant is to directly involve the people closest to your services: your staff and your customers.
3. Any team in any organization in any industry can implement this approach to continuously achieve their optimal potential. (Yes, even yours!)

As a team leader (or an aspiring one), you are in the position to effectively drive these outcomes for your team. Regardless of how the bizarre managed-care industry stumbles around in the coming years, you can unite your team in building the healthcare scenario of your dreams.

When your team is on the same page regarding the mission, vision, and values of your organization, you have everyone aiming for the same outcome. When everyone on your team is working together to effectively balance the staff experience, the patient experience, and the operational/financial dynamics that move you all toward your shared goals, then you are far more likely to achieve outcomes that grow your impact. When you involve your team members in how to meaningfully engage those you serve, consistently exceed expectations for every situation, and creatively leverage the limited resources available, then you position yourselves for magic—even without any pixie dust!

Your outcomes, operational results, culture, reputation, and day-to-day staff and patient experiences are all either by design or by default. World-class organizations never (ever!) settle for "default" determining their future. And neither should you. Your personal legacy should be on purpose, not by accident. You, your colleagues, and your patients deserve optimal results. This book includes proven strategies and tactical tools to help you accomplish that.

That said, no matter where you are right now, there is legitimate hope and opportunities to create a better future. I'm personally encouraged by this quote from F. Scott Fitzgerald:

> For what it's worth: it's never too late or, in my case, too early to be whoever you want to be. There's no time limit, stop whenever you

> want. You can change or stay the same, there are no rules to this thing. We can make the best or the worst of it. I hope you make the best of it. And I hope you see things that startle you. I hope you feel things you never felt before. I hope you meet people with a different point of view. I hope you live a life you're proud of. If you find that you're not, I hope you have the courage to start all over again.

All it takes is a little courage, some guidance (provided in this book), and just enough energy and commitment to start. Yes, making time to plan improvements seems impossible when you are scrambling just to get through each day. But what is the alternative? Settling for less—forever? Thinking that you are too busy to try is like saying you're "too busy driving to stop and get gas". Eventually, your circumstances will *force* you to stop—and that is always a much worse problem. Don't fall into the "nice idea, but I'll need to wait to try until things get less hectic" crowd. Draw a line in the sand and take the first step.

Today.

You can't think your way to a better team. Just planning what to do won't make it a reality. Mere team meetings won't improve your outcomes. The only approach that actually gets results is *doing*. Taking action. Trial and error. Trying again. And again. When every step makes you better—even a little bit, even when all you've learned is what *not* to do—you make progress. And eventually, you optimize your results, making a difference in the things that matter most.

The implementation section of this book will outline the step-by-step team-improvement process that world-class organizations (including leading hospitals) currently use to dominate their industry, with relevant tips on how to adapt that approach to your team's healthcare operation.

4

Leader, Heal Thyself

"Our chief want is someone who will inspire us to be what we know we could be."

— Ralph Waldo Emerson

Your Leadership (Not "Theirs") Is the Key to Your Success

I **admit, I'm biased** when it comes to leadership. It's always been a particular passion of mine. During my last 10 years at Disney, I was asked to lead our leadership initiatives. Afterward, leading change in numerous different industries, I realized that every successful change effort is, at its core, rooted in leadership. Not merely the senior leader, but all leaders at every level of the organization. Truly great leadership changes everything for the better.

Here's the big picture when it comes to any change effort: To improve an organization, you must improve the culture. To improve the culture, you must improve the teams. To improve the teams, you must improve the leadership of each team.

That's you.

Yes, there are likely other leaders in your healthcare organization, perhaps at higher levels in the org chart, who have a larger scope of authority and can significantly influence your team's experience. Developing a good relationship of trust and credibility with them will obviously be helpful, but while you work on that, you need to get busy making *the* difference you came to healthcare for—taking care of people who need you most.

Real Leadership Is an Earned Role, Not a Given Title

Noted leadership expert Mark Sanborn once wrote, "Genuine, authentic leadership infuses meaning into your life, because you know that your efforts count and that you are serving the needs of others as well as your own."[13] Anyone can be given the title of leader, but they have to earn the right to be followed.

What traits inspire people to follow you?

I distinctly remember the first time I got promoted to a supervisory position. My new boss got my attention on the first day, saying, "My job is to find someone better than you. Your job is to make sure I can't. Start learning and keep getting better with some urgency and we'll both win." Kind of shocking, for sure, but it has proven to be a truism that has served all areas of my life since.

Constant learning and improving feed directly into any success. You need to master certain skills to make you and others successful. But the reason people follow a leader goes beyond merely having the best solution for a problem. What traits inspire people to follow you?

SELF-EXAM

Which leader made a big impression on you? Most respond: "They cared about me," or "They supported us in being the best we could be." Consider the behaviors that create those impressions and you'll have a checklist for what builds trust and credibility.

---

[13] Sanborn, 2006.

The Mindset of a Leader

"Aut viam inveniam aut faciam."

(Latin for "I shall either find a way or make one.")

Joe Calloway, in his book *The Leadership Mindset,* states, "No two leaders think exactly alike, but there are some easily identifiable things that most great leaders have in common. This is where leadership starts: with mindset."[14] Have you noticed that what people value internally eventually leaks out in their external behaviors? We must stay aware of our mindset and how it influences our behaviors and performance—because it influences our team's attitudes, behaviors, and performance. When we allow our lives to get out of balance or if we permit unhealthy thoughts to contaminate our thinking, it affects our ability to live up to our healthcare calling. To be clear, I do not mean this as "merely speak your desires into the universe and it will move them toward you," fantasy-land nonsense. This is a pragmatic reality: Where you focus your thinking will ultimately guide your actions—and be reflected in your results (or lack of them).

Your effectiveness as a leader is defined by what you pay the most attention to. One of my mentors would often say, "When you think and act like a leader who attracts followers, *then* you're a leader." To earn the role of trusted advisor to your team, assume that your team is paying attention to everything you do—and don't do—and act accordingly. This requires thinking about not only your job responsibilities but those of your team, as well as your organization—and beyond. Developing an effective leadership mindset means thinking more strategically and considering the ripple effect of everything you and your team do. This requires a careful balance of being aware of large-scale issues (organizational and industry trends) and smaller-scale ones (individual needs and emotional well-being).

A great leader is a "multiplier"—someone who develops other people to lead by example, who multiplies value to those they serve, those they work with, and the organization they support. The ability to transition among these different perspectives is an important skill—but as with any skill, it

[14] Calloway, 2019.

can be developed. So it's helpful to know which skills are the most vital to consider.

"If your actions inspire others to dream more, learn more, do more, and become more, you are a leader."

– John Quincy Adams

Regardless of your title, or lack of title, you are absolutely in a position to have a profound impact on your team's culture and outcomes. Helping your team realize your collective potential will become an example for other teams to follow, which will eventually transform your entire healthcare organization. Before we get ahead of ourselves, however, let's begin with getting *you* ready to successfully guide your team to becoming the energized, high-performing, "having fun while saving the day" kind of group you've always wanted.

Leadership Vital Signs: What Matters Most

Countless books have been published on various aspects of leadership. In fact, I learned at a business meeting with Amazon that a search for leadership books on their platform results in more than 60,000 titles—and that about 10 leadership books are added *every day*! Bottom line: None of us can read them all.

As a voracious reader (my wife thinks I have a borderline chemical imbalance), I've read well over a thousand business books over the years. Despite every author creating new leadership topics with trademarked new buzzwords (a pet peeve of mine), most leadership books emphasize just four foundational issues:

1. **Integrity/Being a role model:** Be worth following!
2. **Influence/Engagement:** You need others to accomplish anything significant.
3. **Excellence:** Nothing inspires passion like being the best.
4. **Vision:** Unless you can articulate a compelling goal, no one follows.

To zero in on the most important related leadership considerations, here's an executive summary of each one as a mini-masterclass for you.

Role-Model Leadership

"Example is not the main thing in persuading others; it's the only thing."

— Albert Schweitzer

The word *integrity* comes from a root word meaning "wholeness or completeness." Integrity simply means there is "completeness" between words and deeds. The common phrase *walking the talk* reflects the application of this term in day-to-day living. To have integrity means there is alignment between what you say you value and what you do. A person with integrity is dependable and worthy of trust. A person with integrity is also someone whom others are drawn to for partnership or leadership.

Teams may follow a boss without integrity ... when they are present. But teams only whole-heartedly commit to the cause when a leader models trustworthy behaviors and demonstrates integrity. As C.S. Lewis once famously wrote: "Integrity is doing the right thing, even when no one is watching."

You've likely been deceived by bad leaders in the past. Anyone who is skilled at communicating, especially if they are in a position of power, can fool some people for a time. But no one willingly follows someone for long if they feel they aren't honest.

That doesn't mean you have to be perfect. It just means that you have to be humble in the face of learning. Being a leader is a fascinating and often puzzling dichotomy of being bold yet humble; confident yet not arrogant; guiding yet not overly controlling; compassionate yet holding others (and yourself) accountable.

But one thing is certain: Your team (and everyone else) notices what you do. You are the tone setter, whether you like it or not. Nothing sends a more powerful message than how you spend your time, effort, and money. If you spend most of your time at work interacting with one particular group of people, then you are showing the world that they are your priority.

SELF-EXAM

While at work, how do you spend your time? What does that say about your priorities? What message are you sending others based on how you spend your time? Is it aligned with your intent? If not, how might you improve your actions to better align with what is truly important to you?

You'll become a great leader only by taking action and gaining experience. It's a refining process that never ends. It takes massive amounts of courage and a thick skin. As famed psychologist Viktor Frankl once said, "What is to give light must endure burning." The key to enduring is to strengthen your level of commitment to the goal and your sincere care for those you lead. Philosopher Nietzsche said it best: "He who has a why to live for can bear almost any how."

Bottom line: If you want to become a more effective leader, commit yourself to caring more about your mission and your team to overcome any challenges.

Becoming a Trusted Advisor

The term *trusted advisor* has been around for decades. It is typically used in a sales-related context, but I'm convinced it is a relevant goal for all leaders (anyone who can influence their culture). This valuable concept quickly became one of the foundational building blocks in our Performance Excellence initiative.

We've all experienced what it is like to work with someone who lacks one (or, if you're unfortunate, both) of these traits. Even if they are extremely capable of delivering extraordinary results regarding the technical aspects of their job (time and/or resource management, process management, etc.), if they are not trustworthy, it is difficult to follow them without frequently hesitating. If, on the other hand, they have proven to be very trustworthy and sincerely have your best interest at heart, but they are inconsistent or can't function effectively with the other technical aspects of their job, it is painful to follow them when the experience will likely fall short of everyone's expectations.

Figure 4-1 models the two primary facets of leadership:

1. The ability to achieve results, which provides credibility to accomplish the mission within the available resources.
2. The alignment of relationship-building behaviors with the organizational culture, which supports the mission, vision, and values of that culture. That is, do others trust that you support them in a caring manner?

Figure 4-1: Team Accountability Matrix

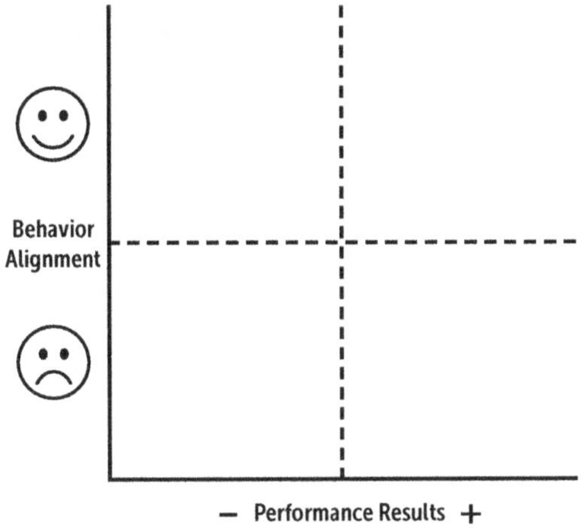

This model helps guide attention toward the relationship between the two and the natural consequences of each combination. World-class results are impossible when you excuse or allow sub-world-class behaviors or results. The goal is to develop yourself and each member of your team to demonstrate both skills in the top-right quadrant. Table 4-1 has more details for each part of this helpful model.

Table 4-1. The Team Accountability Matrix

Combination	Consequences	Response
Misaligned Behavior and Poor Performance Results *(bottom left)*	Anyone who is failing in both categories is toxic to the organization. Drastic improvement is required, quickly. Permitting this behavior undermines any motivation for the rest of the team. Why should they make an extra effort to excel if this person isn't held accountable?	Insist on dramatic improvements toward company norms, and an intense effort to identify the glaring gap between goals and performance.
Misaligned Behavior and Positive Performance Results *(bottom right)*	Most common with technically skilled team members who don't see the value of engaging others to create a unified team. Short-term, results-only efforts undermine long-term sustainability.	Help them see how their poor behaviors and interpersonal communication affect workplace relationships, undermining the potential of the rest of the team/organization.
Aligned Behaviors & Poor Performance Results *(top left)*	Typically, this person is a beloved member of the team. Often passionate about the brand and the people, they can sometimes fall short in delivering the consistent results you strive for.	To keep someone so valuably supportive of the culture, emphasize remedial training in the skill required or transfer to a different better-fit skills position.
Aligned Behaviors and Positive Performance Results *(top right)*	This is the combination that achieves long-term world-class excellence. They exhibit all the relational skills that reinforce a healthy, supportive culture and the skills to generate growth and mission success.	Recognize and reward the behaviors and share the outcomes with others on the team as an example of how, in the same environment, the goals of culture and results can be successfully achieved.

Where Clinical Magic is Happening: Tampa General Hospital

Tampa General Hospital Facebook post, September 1, 2022: "Our Neuro ICU was excited to welcome John Couris, Tampa General Hospital President & CEO, and Phil Dingle, Chairman of the Board, for shadowing yesterday! John and Phil not only worked alongside our physicians, advanced practice providers, and nurses, but also spent time with a few of our patients and their families.

Every month, John and Phil suit up in scrubs and shadow a new unit for a real day-in-the-life experience as a team member

> working the halls of TGH. It's this hands-on work that allows them to connect with team members, learn new skills, and discover ways to even better support our world-class team. Thanks for stopping by! #WeAreTGH"

Becoming an Influential Leader

"A leader without followers is just someone out taking a walk."

– Unknown

The ability to influence is another key characteristic of a world-class leader. Whether you have staff who report directly to you or you are an individual contributor, your ability to accomplish superior results as a clinical professional rests primarily on your ability to influence the many others needed to tactically execute the operation.

It has been said that adding relationship skills to the characteristics of integrity, excellence, and vision is what creates influence. Expressing a compelling vision, along with understanding others and what motivates them, is a critical factor in influencing them—regardless of what level of formal power you may yield in the situation.

My team created a tool (Table 4-2) to help leaders increase their influence with those they strategically need to partner with. I feel obligated to first say, only half joking, that this is not a tool intended to help you manipulate someone. Any tool can be used for good or evil, so stay true to your values and, as a role-model leader, proceed with integrity—and in good conscience.

That said, the first question you need to ask yourself is, "Does this person trust me?" Before you can hope to influence someone, they must be confident that you have their best interests at heart. Sometimes, this means you must invest time and effort in proving your trustworthiness with them—and it may take weeks or months before your relationship is at a place where they are willing to believe your intent.

There's no short-cut. You simply need to do the work. (Start ASAP!)

Secondly, you must objectively assess how capable you are in *their* mind. Perhaps you need to improve your skills before being considered credible in their eyes. If you legitimately have the expertise needed to deliver results, then the solution may be pursuing ways to make that person aware. Spotlighting your capabilities isn't bragging if it helps others make better decisions for their benefit.

Influence requires the foundation of trust and credibility. Without them both, you are wasting time and energy—and possibly creating a "forced" element to your relationship that can fester and make things even worse. There's no sustainable way to fake it. You must be committed to developing yourself, nurturing the relationship, and earning it. When it comes to building leadership influence, you can't rush it. Human nature doesn't work that way. There's an old saying: "The best time to plant a tree is 20 years ago. The second-best time to plant a tree is today." Save yourself unnecessary trouble and invest in building your influence and future effectiveness the right way. Today.

Once you have sufficiently developed your levels of trust and credibility, the next step of growing your influence is to identify their personal priorities. Everyone has certain things they value most. Look for clues; people react passionately to topics they care most about. One way to combat the massive amount of distracting "noise" we all must deal with every day is to strategically break through with more meaningful communication (which is 90 percent action and 10 percent words). If you properly reference one of their priority issues in connection to the new course of action you want to pursue, you will likely get more attention than if you simply make the request amid all the other competing demands for their attention.

Influence requires the foundation of trust and credibility.

Finally, an important consideration to influencing others is regarding the person's goals in relation to what you want to recommend. How can you help *them* win? Discover what areas of agreement or disagreement are between the two of you. Look for ways to collaborate with them to resolve the issues so you become a team by attacking the problem together. People are more likely to support an ally who has supported them in meaningful efforts.

Table 4-2 is a tool to help you strategically develop your influencing opportunities.

Table 4-2. Influence Implementation Tool

Person to Influence	1.	2.	3.
What level of trust does this person have in you? What can you do to enhance it?			
What level of credibility do you have with this person? What can you do to improve it?			
What do they care most about? (Reputation? Power? Quality?)			
What areas of agreement and/or disagreement are there? How can you collaboratively help this person win? How do you want them to feel?			
What actions will achieve success for these considerations?			

For example, after establishing trust and credibility, you could approach the decision maker you want to influence and say something like "[Person], I've been noticing there's been a decline in [problem], which is really undermining *our* team's [person's priority issue]. According to [evidence you've gathered], we could do [recommended solution]. How can *we* [verbally aligning the two of you as partners in this effort] work together to confront this [problem] and restore our team's [person's priority issue]?"

Bottom line: Accomplishing anything of significance requires working well with others. Effective (and appropriate) influence is the way to earn support and cooperation in overcoming the healthcare challenges you face.

Top Leadership-Excellence Skills

The goal of excellence is valuable not only from a leadership skills standpoint, but also from the perspective that no one on your team will develop any passion about mediocre goals. It is human nature to gravitate toward being part of an endeavor that achieves superior, extraordinary outcomes. Let's begin with what constitutes leadership excellence.

No team improvement effort can happen without some kind of guidance from a leader—whether a formal leader or an informal one. Given that effective leadership directly influences the effectiveness of team performance (and patient outcomes), it's important to explore what abilities make the biggest impact. According to the hundreds of leadership books, assessments, and operational engagements I've been exposed to over the past 40 years, here is the generally agreed upon short list:

- Consistently role models our mission, vision, values, and culture: Essentially, do you walk the talk?
- Shares compelling vision and clearly defined goal setting: Keeping the team on target and committed will make it more likely that each day they will move closer toward that goal.
- Communicates honestly and effectively, informing and listening: These are the foundations of trustworthiness.
- Encourages individual involvement and teamwork: The better you are at generating involvement, the more you will get buy-in and ownership.
- Holds themselves and others accountable for exceeding expectations: Accountability puts effort and resources toward what is most important.
- Recognizes and rewards results and encourages sharing insights: Reinforcing effective behaviors makes them much more likely to be repeated.
- Develops others' potential for professional success: The team's overall development depends on the amount of collective individual development.
- Delivers effective planning and creative problem solving: Your

capacity to provide an environment conducive to innovation determines how innovative and agile the team can be.

- Demonstrates strategic and fair decision making: Ensure that the myriad decisions made throughout a process are aligned for relational effectiveness and long-term success.
- Provides administrative coordination and time management: Optimizing the resource of time creates efficiency.

As you can see, these "most important" competencies cover a wide variety of skills. At first glance, all this detail seems a bit overwhelming. One helpful way to view this list is to notice that all of these competencies can be simplified into two primary categories: building relationships and generating results (the Team Accountability Matrix). Interestingly, the number of skills mentioned for relationship building is more than double the number of results-focused skills. The most effective team leaders find a way to hold themselves, and others on their team, accountable for both. In other words, as introduced earlier, they become a trusted advisor.

PRO TIP

Use the word *yet* more often—and more strategically. It can turn the phrase "I don't know what to do" into "I don't know what to do ... yet." "I'm not good enough" becomes "I'm not good enough ... yet." Numerous leaders I've coached over the years have shared that this was a big transformative approach to stepping into the unknown—and building the confidence to try to learn their way to success. Make *yet* part of your first steps toward becoming the leader you want to be!

BONUS PRO TIP

Several of these leadership skills are involved with the most common causes of team conflict: insufficient clarity regarding expectations, roles, and responsibilities. Before embarking on any new task, ensure those details are crystal clear and you'll avoid most of the potential problems down the road.

Table 4-3 is a quick sample of a leadership assessment that reflects the key indicators included in nearly all popular assessments out there. Simply follow the key behaviors on the left, rate yourself in the next column, and then document anything you could stop or start doing to improve your effectiveness in each issue.

Table 4-3. Sample Leadership Assessment

Behavior	Rating 1–10	Practical Improvement Actions	
Consistently Role Models Our Mission, Vision, Values, and Culture		Stop	
		Start	
Shares Compelling Vision and Clearly Defined Goal Setting		Stop	
		Start	
Communicates Honestly and Effectively, Informing and Listening		Stop	
		Start	
Encourages Individual Involvement and Teamwork		Stop	
		Start	
Holds Themselves and Others Accountable for Exceeding Expectations		Stop	
		Start	
Recognizes and Rewards Results and Encourages Sharing Insights		Stop	
		Start	
Develops Others' Potential for Professional Success		Stop	
		Start	

Behavior	Rating 1–10	Practical Improvement Actions	
Demonstrates Effective Planning and Creative Problem Solving		Stop	
		Start	
Demonstrates Strategic and Fair Decision Making		Stop	
		Start	
Provides Administrative Coordination and Time Management		Stop	
		Start	

Once you complete your self-assessment, the real progress starts by requesting your *team* to individually rate you. Ask them to identify the most important abilities for your unique team circumstances at this time, then provide constructive feedback about each behavior. Gaining insight into how your team rates you for each, and *why*, is the leadership "hack" to getting better at the particular behaviors that matter most.

At world-class organizations, every successful improvement initiative begins with preparing the people needed to lead or influence that effort—at every level of the organization.

SELF-EXAM

How proficient are you in each of these leadership skills? Start with identifying the three to five most important abilities for your role (or a role you aspire to). Highlight any of the recommendations in the previous content, then reach out to anyone you know who is skilled at that trait and can provide improvement insights. Search the internet or any other resource you have access to and establish an action plan to develop yourself. Investing in your own leadership capabilities will pay dividends throughout the rest of your career—and benefit your private life as well!

The Bigger Perspective of Performance Excellence

The goal or vision of the future must be compelling enough to justify extraordinary effort from your team. Ideally, your vision is well grounded in your organization's values, a future state that excites your team with vastly improved benefits connected to what they care most about and that is *just* beyond their grasp—which will spark a desire to start and achieve as soon as possible. Planning how to approach your team with a call to improve can be an intimidating situation, because you are sharing a strong personal opinion. Let's introduce some of the broader aspects of painting a mental picture of what the future can hold for those who join your improvement crusade.

Here are some quick tips for developing and communicating a compelling change vision:

- Identify a goal that is intriguing and exciting, but just out of the team's current ability. Ensure that every person on your team can visualize how it affects their personal role.
- Describe the contrast between the current unsatisfactory circumstances and the desired scenario, particularly how it could positively affect your patients and the team.
- Consider what words would best describe the ultimate realization of the improvement effort. Work to identify language that elicits a positive emotional response.
- Be clear and concise; aim for 10–30 seconds to share and explain. Avoid jargon or buzzwords, which will undermine your message.

Ask yourself:

- What matters most to this team? Why did they get into healthcare?
- What is the real problem we want to solve? What is so frustrating?
- What is the preferred way that this team should be operating? (This connects to question one, or what matters most to them.)

Your change vision shouldn't include solutions; just describe the future state and the confidence that, together, you can make things better. Remember:

Each person must have an opportunity to participate in creating the solution, or there will be no buy-in, ownership, or lasting engagement.

> *"One important key to success is self-confidence. An important key to self-confidence is preparation."*
>
> **– Arthur Ashe**

Setting the Stage for Your Breakthrough

As the team leader, you'll need to prepare yourself, and then your team, to begin your improvement initiative. The upcoming chapters include the tools you'll need to implement the following key steps in unifying your team in this effort. Consider the following bigger-picture goals as a preview for beginning your preparation as you progress through the rest of this book:

- Share your vision and belief in the culture.
- Share your enthusiasm for and pride in the organization.
- Energize others with your commitment to optimal performance.
- Display decisiveness and a sense of urgency in achieving goals.
- Encourage creativity and risk taking.
- Promote teamwork to accomplish your team's and organization's business objectives.
- Set challenging goals that are realistic, clear, and measurable.
- Hold yourself and other team members accountable for performance.
- Unleash the potential of each team member by providing developmental opportunities.
- Listen intently to diverse opinions.
- Communicate honestly and frequently, soliciting feedback and suggestions from team members at all levels of the organization.
- Inject a sense of humor, fun, and enjoyment into your work.
- Set the stage and work with others to improve the patient experience.
- Celebrate the victories!

As a leader, your objective is to bring all these important details together to achieve the improvement goals your team shares, but it won't happen by accident. Balancing your focus on inner team workings and external outcomes is tricky, but the results are worth it. David Harris, chief operating officer for Spear Physical Therapy, puts it this way:[15]

> As a leader, it's not only the retention, but also the productivity side of it. If you have your people's full buy-in, and you fully buy into them, then your bottom line takes care of itself. Yes, you have those performance metrics out there, that, if you really look at them, the bottom line is they all relate back to the culture of the team, and the culture relates back to the vision, mission, and values. And those are just words on paper if you're not living them out. Any company has to be very careful about that. We must demonstrate these values, to inspire people to reach their full potential. If you're not living it, you're going to crumble from within. You'll see higher turnover rates. You'll see less buy-in for new ideas. Help the patient, help the consumers, help the folks coming onto your team. I think for long-term success in healthcare, we must keep people in mind.

PRO TIP

Providing guidance and formative feedback is a particularly important skill for leading a team. One effective way to create a more accepting mindset from those you need to share feedback with is to set a context of why you are initiating this conversation and encourage them to act. For example: "I'm sharing my feedback because I have very high expectations, and I'm confident that you can reach them" (in your own words, of course.)

[15] Harris, 2019.

Leaving a Legacy—For Good...or Bad

Ask yourself, "What is my motivation for striving to be an extraordinary leader?" Money, fame, and power may be enticing, but aren't very aligned with making a difference—especially if you have a heart for helping people in healthcare. Maintaining awareness of what matters most to you can sustain you through the inevitable difficulties of your sometimes-intense calling.

Once, during a healthcare-system consulting project, my client was struggling with how bureaucratic and cumbersome their operations had become. Over years of growth, they had added reams of policies and procedures, and had set up the organizational structure as a complicated matrix—which had stalled their progress and created vulnerability in their marketplace. As my team and I navigated the assessment process, I had several informative conversations with people at all levels of the company. I quickly noticed a trend among the different divisions: When I asked about who they thought was the most dependable, trustworthy, and capable person in the organization, most identified a mid-level manager who worked for a function that interacted with most of the divisions. Out of curiosity, I asked if he would meet with me to discuss his opinions about the challenges they all faced. Upon entering his office to discuss his insights, I was struck by a handwritten note he had pinned on the wall. He explained that he'd made it as part of a workshop he had attended years prior, when he was tasked with identifying his "secret sauce" to success. It read:

"*Do* stuff. Be *good* at the stuff you do. Do stuff that *matters*. Do stuff *with* others. Do stuff *for* others."

> *Do* stuff. Be *good* at the stuff you do. Do stuff that *matters*. Do stuff *with* others. Do stuff *for* others.

He said posting that simple reminder made his decisions easier and kept him focused on what matters most in life.

That simple handwritten note became the guide for streamlining their operations and setting the stage for their remarkable turnaround.

Part of your quest for success during your career will be fine-tuning your personal "secret sauce." Identifying what matters most and makes the difference you want to make in alignment with your unique personality will be a tremendous breakthrough for you—and will lead to the next breakthrough, and the next. As a team leader, no matter how far up the corporate ladder you go, this process will always involve other people.

I recall an experience that cemented this insight for me. One day, I received an invitation to a retirement party for someone I had led years prior. I hadn't seen Dan in about a decade and knew I would enjoy catching up with numerous other guests as well, so I was eager to attend.

After arriving at his house and enjoying the initial mingling, I found myself with a group in Dan's study, where I came across a framed, handwritten notecard made out to him. The note recognized him for making a vital difference in an important project, and it was signed by me! I was surprised—not just because it was hanging on a wall in his office, but because I couldn't, for the life of me, remember giving him that note.

I walked over to Dan and asked him about the framed note, joking that I thought he had hung it on the wall knowing that I would see it. He assured me that wasn't the case, and then called his 4-year-old grandson over. He said, "Tell Mr. Mark what that is." His young grandson suddenly got a big smile on his face, straightened up, and proudly told me, "That's what Grandpa's work thinks of Grandpa ... and they love him!" I was shocked! Dan explained that he'd been going through a particularly frustrating time at work and had been seriously considering leaving the company. I just happened to approach him and remind him of the difference he was making and that I noticed. I even told him (evidently) to take the rest of the day off and take his wife on a surprise date to the movies (with tickets I enclosed, according to the note) because I knew that was a favorite pastime of theirs and that she had sacrificed time with him during the many overtime hours he had been working. Dan finished by thanking me and explaining that it was my personal recognition that had turned his attitude around and convinced him to stay, working 15 more satisfying years before retiring.

I learned a very important lesson from this humbling encounter. This was particularly significant to me because my personality is not touchy-feely. I have always struggled with the relationship side of being a leader, but recognizing that they are vital to success, I've sought out tools (some of which I'm sharing with you in this book) and tested them out, adapting them to what works for me. Constantly improving your leadership engagement makes a difference—sometimes in the most unexpected of ways.

Making a difference doesn't require much more than sincerely connecting with a personal gesture. By recognizing the link between a person's behavior and the impact it makes on your team (bringing the organization's values to life, exceeding the expectations of the people your team serves, supporting those on the team in delivering excellence, etc.), you reinforce that behavior. I'm not talking about some corny, fake, scripted words. Use the "real" ways you naturally talk among your team. Communicate how you feel in words that align with your culture and circumstances. The important thing is to stop overthinking and *do* it.

I must admit, my early attempts at recognition were awkward, and I made some missteps. Given that I'm more of a results guy, I tried to overcompensate by committing to formally recognizing at least three of my staff per week to improve my engagement. One time, because I'm an avid reader, I started handing out copies of my favorite business book as recognition gifts, but I soon discovered (after a few strained but polite looks and fake smiles) that my team didn't always value books as much as I did. Another lesson learned. To up my game on how to best do this whole recognition thing (and save money on wasted books), I developed a helpful tool that might be a good place to start:

Strategic Reinforcement Cards. Make a list of all the people on your team. Create a card or document for each staff member (I'm low-tech, so I use 3x5 cards) with the name of the person at the top. I then note all the ways that they are valuable to the team, the organization, or me (to include current projects, etc.) and make a list. Next, I begin learning more about each person, particularly what they enjoy as hobbies, favorite foods/restaurants, and other ways that they like to have fun, recording those details on the flip side of the card. The result is that I now have a list of things to recognize each person for and how they are likely to prefer being rewarded, which makes the effort far more personal and relevant to them. The only thing missing now is to spot when each person has done something notable and recognize them in person.

PRO TIP

Brag about your team member to your boss in an email, then share that with them afterward.

BONUS PRO TIP

Ask your boss to personally congratulate the team member directly. Extra points if in front of the rest of your team.

If you can give a (hopefully relevant) gift, then great. If not, that's okay. The most important aspect is the sincerity of your appreciation. Make it real. Connect to something legitimately earned. In addition to reinforcing the effective behaviors, you'll also reinforce your working relationship. Respect comes from walking your talk with integrity. This becomes an easy win.

Preparing to Lead Real Improvement

Bookshelves are also fully stocked with advice on common leadership challenges like communication and strategy. Some tips are practical, but most only sound good in theory. I've made sure to include those that have worked for organizational-transformation efforts I've personally participated in, which usually happened in hectic, high-pressure, real-world environments like yours.

Person-to-person interaction is vital to any team's success. Using effective communication is important, but here's the human-nature hiccup: People won't tell you the truth unless they trust you and want you to succeed. The solution? You must develop a good relationship with them first—then work on the mechanics of communication, and so forth.

PRO TIP

Start your preparation by clarifying *why* taking action is important to *you.* Make it personal to make it compelling. Describe in one minute or less why it must happen. Follow this template:

1. Purpose: We all want [*the meaningful, compelling goal*], but 2. Problem: the reality is not [*what we should settle for*]. 3. Priority: This issue matters to me because [*I'm confident that we can do better and that we all deserve to make it easier to achieve excellence*]. 4. Potential: Together, we are capable of figuring out practical ways to realize [*our potential*] and make our future work easier. 5. Participate: Would you be willing to [*work with me*] and explore possibilities?

Having your message clarified will help you convince others you've thought it through and are committed to effective improvements.

As you craft your plan to transform your team and their results, seriously consider enlisting your boss to support the improvements you are aiming for. Do your best to ensure that they visibly back you in your efforts. Invite them to attend your team meetings every so often, where they can make it clear that they value the team's efforts to optimize their potential—and that your efforts as a team leader will be supported in the months to come. This clarity helps erase most second thoughts your team may have about the proposed changes.

If you're new to a team, or if you simply want to make the team dynamic new, let them know what about the job is important to you and what you expect. Then, create opportunities for each team member to get to know you (and you to know them), and trust and support you. Earn that trust and support by supporting and developing them in ways that benefit them in alignment with their personal values and goals, and the values and goals of your organization.

It's almost impossible to lead a team you don't understand. That's why you'll get a fantastic Team-Leader Alignment tool in Chapter 6 to help you with this effort. You should know why each person on your team specifically cares about the healthcare field. Your team should know why you care about being in healthcare. They should also know why you care about them. Connecting with one another on why you all choose to do what you do opens many doors to improve communication, support, engagement, and outcomes. Remaining in the dark creates significant disadvantages. Again, the choice is yours.

What's Your Treatment of Choice?

The stereotype of Disney is that it's a fantasy world "where dreams magically come true." The behind-the-scenes reality is that a rigorous operational methodology creates those "magical" results. This is the same for virtually every world-class organization. From the outside, their success almost seems like they must have some secret trick or unattainable advantage. In truth, when you examine how they accomplish their fantastic achievements, it comes down to a group of people, promising to help other people, and working effectively together to deliver on that promise. Clearing away the distractions and embracing the methods that have been proven to deliver those results are the shortcuts we all hope for.

> You can absolutely influence these circumstances by applying the proven approach and tools in this book.

So far, we've reviewed the nature of change and how to overcome common obstacles. I've showcased the approach to world-class excellence that virtually all leading organizations (yes, even healthcare) follow. I've emphasized preparation tips for how you as a leader can best influence the overall effort. The rest of this book details the implementation process and provides practical tools for you to lead your team to the results that you need to achieve your goal of healthcare excellence.

Author William Ward once said, "The pessimist complains about the wind; the optimist expects it to change; the realist adjusts the sails." You have a decision to make. Despite what you've experienced with previous change efforts—crushing failures, occasional victories, and everything in between—you and your team face a significant crossroads in healthcare. You can absolutely influence these circumstances by applying the proven approach and tools in this book. Will you passively stand by and take whatever others chose for you, or will you be the heroic catalyst for the breakthrough you and your team deserve?

Change is already happening all around you. You are in the position to influence any changes into legitimate improvements for you, your team, your organization, and, most important, the patients in your care. It's time to start up or give up. Either give this book to someone who actually wants to improve things or kick off the step-by-step process of finally achieving your and your team's potential—and maybe even spark breakthroughs in other parts of your healthcare organization!

SECTION THREE

Prepare Your Team

5

First Things First—The Missing Link

Consider this: When you left work to go home yesterday, did you get where you intended? This rhetorical question seems a bit silly, but it points out an often-overlooked insight. You got where you were going because you clearly identified the destination in advance and made decisions along the way that resulted in progress toward that goal. Imagine if your planned route was unexpectedly blocked—would that stop you from getting home? Would you just stay at the impasse until the circumstances changed? Not likely. You would simply try a different route—but only an option that helped you make progress toward your goal: home. Anything else would be counterproductive (and a waste of gas). What determines the "best" route? It depends on your end goal, options, and resources.

The same is true for making progress as a team. Unless there is a clear north star to guide you, chances are, you won't easily get to where you want to be. And you can't get there unless you know where "there" is!

There are numerous reasons a team may realize outcomes that are below their potential. When teams don't have a compelling goal, they won't invest extra effort to move toward it. When teams are unclear about how to get there, they hesitate and are slow to commit.

Are you consistently achieving your aspiration to provide hope and compassionate care to those in need? You may have seen some symptoms of not clearly guiding your team: ineffective communication; conflicting priorities; everyone focused on busywork, merely putting out the same fires every day, with no significant improvement or growth.

Thankfully, transforming your team (and, ultimately, your organization) doesn't require an expensive and traumatic overhaul. It simply begins with a recalibration of the tools that provide the foundation of how you work together effectively. I refer to these as your "core non-negotiables." Generally speaking, they include your:

- Mission: Why your team exists; your purpose
- Vision: Where your team needs to go
- Values: How your team needs to behave in alignment with what is important

Just how vital are these non-negotiables? When the late Tony Hsieh, founder of the revered online shoe company Zappos.com, was asked what he'd do differently if he could restart his company from scratch, he responded by saying, "If I could go back and do Zappos all over again, I would actually come up with our values from day one."[16]

Yes, values are important, but I'd like to add this clarification: It's not the company values that transform organizations; it is the values of the people that transform the behaviors and outcomes.

After Microsoft merged with LinkedIn, the latter company's CEO, Jeff Weiner, said, "Every day I come to work, I'm primarily guided by two things: First, realizing our mission and vision. The second thing I focus on every day is making our culture and values come to life."[17]

Obviously, these renowned leaders have a valuable, experienced perspective on creating a thriving organization. For any organization to thrive, their teams need to thrive. The great thing is that, with the right tools, you can influence and lead your team to optimize their potential (and possibly serve as the catalyst for an organization-wide transformation—but let's not get ahead of ourselves).

Over the years, I've noticed that most change programs fail because leaders either overanalyze (as an excuse to never take risky action) or

---

[16] Montini, 2014.

[17] Microsoft News Center, 2016.

rush into a course of action before considering the root cause of the subpar performance or the real criteria for success. In other words, they skip past using the core non-negotiables in order to get to the good stuff. This misguided shortcut inevitably leads to initial confusion, then maybe some short-term gains, followed by regressing to business as usual and no improvement to show for all the time and effort. The dreaded "Program of the Month" curse!

To bypass all that needless frustration, successful teams invest time to study and understand the core non-negotiables and their impact on team and organizational culture, and strategically leverage them for sustainable improvements that matter.

"The key to good decision making is not knowledge. It is understanding. We are swimming in the former. We are desperately lacking in the latter."

– Malcolm Gladwell

Organize or Agonize

In his book, *The Ride of a Lifetime,* Disney CEO Bob Iger went so far as to state the following: "A company's culture is shaped by a lot of things, but this is one of the most important—you have to convey your priorities clearly and repeatedly," and "'You can do a lot for the morale of the people around you (and therefore the people around them) just by taking the guesswork out of their day-to-day life."[18] This isn't just for executives and corporations. Any team leader can leverage these tools to create the same culture and results.

Across various best-in-class organizations, one thing becomes clear: Once non-negotiables are clarified and agreed upon, every decision afterward is made more easily. Resources are more prudently utilized. Internal teamwork gets more unified. Patient experiences become more consistent. There's less frustration and anxiety all around. Everyone wins.

Imagine how your workplace could improve—and what it could mean for everyone involved.

---

[18] Iger, 2019.

When you create the tools needed to serve mission (the map), the vision (the destination), and values (the agreed-upon ways to work together to get to the goal), you unify the team and make it far easier to achieve your shared goals.

A client once had a great insight: She likened the process of developing your non-negotiables to picking hiking boots for walking the grueling, 2,000-mile Appalachian Trail. You'll be using your boots heavily throughout the experience, so if you don't invest the time to make sure you get ones that fit you well and are suitable for the months-long journey, chances are your experience will be miserable, and you'll quit before you reach your destination. Every successful person attempting that kind of feat knows that the basic task of selecting the right hiking boots is invaluable!

Once non-negotiables are clarified and agreed upon, every decision afterward is made more easily.

So how does this translate to healthcare? In his book *Why We Work*, psychologist Barry Schwartz shared research that included insights related to the healthcare industry.[19] He described a study of what creates work satisfaction, and the primary indicator was not pay, but meaningful responsibilities. Healthcare jobs were ranked at the top of all industries, but *only* for those employees whose roles were connected beyond the tasks of their job description to the higher purpose—the mission, vision, and values.

An example Schwartz mentioned was one particular healthcare role: hospital custodian/environmental services. He shared the following comments about the research interviews:[20]

> Luke works as a custodian in a major teaching hospital. His job description says nothing about responsibility or care for patients

[19] Schwartz, 2015a.

[20] Schwartz, 2015b.

> and their families. He has a long list of duties, including to "collect and dispose of soiled linen" and "stock restroom supplies," but not a single item on the list even mentions interacting with another human being. From the description, Luke could be working in a shoe factory or a mortuary instead of a hospital. His "official" duties were only one part of his real job.
>
> But Luke was doing a different job than his official description would suggest, as researcher Amy Wrzesniewski discovered when she and her team conducted in-depth interviews with Luke and other hospital custodians. The researchers asked the custodians to talk about their jobs, and the custodians began to tell them stories about what they did. Luke's stories told them that his "official" duties were only one part of his real job, and that another central part of his job was to make the patients and their families feel comfortable, to cheer them up when they were down, to encourage them and divert them from their pain and their fear, and to give them a willing ear if they felt like talking. Luke wanted to do something more than mere custodial work.

Schwartz explained that, because the hospital expanded the team's perception of their more important purpose, their personal "why" and resulting satisfaction far exceeded the limited tasks determined by their functional responsibilities. "They were not generic custodians; they were hospital custodians. They saw themselves as playing an important role in an institution whose aim is to see to the care and welfare of patients ... Virtually any job has the potential to offer people satisfaction."

Being in the healthcare field makes it easy to connect your day-to-day activities with your higher calling. In fact, when speaking at the 2018 Federation of the Boards of Nursing Professions, Pope Francis made the following comments:[21]

> Being in contact with physicians and family members, in addition to the sick, you become, in hospitals, in healthcare facilities, and in homes, the crossroads of a thousand relationships, which require attention, competence, and compassion ... Before the uniqueness

---

[21] Pope Francis, 2018.

> of each situation, indeed, it is never enough to follow a protocol, but a constant—and tiresome—effort of discernment and attention to the individual person is required. All this makes your profession a veritable mission and makes you 'experts in humanity.

No matter your role, you are part of an organization that provides healing, care, and hope to those who are most vulnerable. This is something to be very proud of! But humans need reminding—and tools that guide bringing those fantastic values to life.

Clarifying Your Non-Negotiables

This aspect of setting your team up for success is so important, I want to include some examples about how to understand core non-negotiables and how to use them once you've identified the right ones for your team. But before I start sharing those insider details, I want to make a couple of things clear, which will (hopefully) decrease any anxiety about taking on this task:

- You most likely won't have to make up anything from scratch, so relax! *Really!*
- There's a 99 percent chance that your organization already has established purpose, mission, vision, and values. Usually, they show up during your orientation program. In some instances, they'll be on a wall, or maybe even on a laminated card or badge. Very rarely will they be already integrated into all your operational processes and team standard operating procedures.
- The good news for you is, if you have access to any of these, you and your team merely need to translate them into behaviors and goals that are relevant for your team's unique function.
- Yes, this is critically important, but I've got your back. We'll just do a quick overview and then get to a step-by-step approach that teams at world-class organizations do to thrive—even in difficult times.

Okay, here's an executive summary of the core non-negotiables with some healthcare examples. Note the differences in style and tone and how they align with the personality of the organization they represent:

Mission: "To Do"

A mission statement is meant to describe why you exist and what you intend to do to realize your ultimate purpose. Ideally, your mission reflects what your business is all about to those you serve—your patients, employees, and community.

Table 5-1 includes some examples.

Table 5-1. Mission Examples

Organization	Mission
Mayo Clinic	To inspire hope and contribute to health and well-being by providing the best care to every patient through integrated clinical practice, education and research
St. Jude Children's Research Hospital	The mission of St. Jude Children's Research Hospital is to advance cures, and means of prevention, for pediatric catastrophic diseases through research and treatment. Consistent with the vision of our founder Danny Thomas, no child is denied treatment based on race, religion or a family's ability to pay.
Cleveland Clinic	Caring for life, researching for health, educating those who serve.
University of Texas MD Anderson Cancer Center	To eliminate cancer in Texas, the nation, and the world through outstanding programs that integrate patient care, research and prevention, and through education for undergraduate and graduate students, trainees, professionals, employees and the public.
Massachusetts General Hospital	Guided by the needs of our patients and their families, we aim to deliver the very best health care in a safe, compassionate environment; to advance that care through innovative research and education; and to improve the health and well-being of the diverse communities we serve.
Tampa General Hospital	We heal. We teach. We innovate. Care for everyone. Every day.
AdventHealth Hospital	Extending the Healing Ministry of Christ

SELF-EXAM

Consider your organization's mission statement. How might you reword it to be most relevant for your functional team?

Vision: "To Be"

The vision statement is intended to be the company's north star, serving to provide direction to all parts of the organization. The vital part of the vision is providing orientation at any given time to navigate through any circumstances. Ideally, it should describe a future status that the entire workforce wants, in a way that inspires passion.

Table 5-2 includes some examples.

Table 5-2. Vision Examples

Organization	Vision
Mayo Clinic	Mayo Clinic will provide an unparalleled experience as the most trusted partner for health care.
St. Jude Children's Research Hospital	To accelerate progress against catastrophic disease at a global level
Cleveland Clinic	Our vision for Cleveland Clinic is to be the best place for care anywhere and the best place to work in healthcare.
University of Texas MD Anderson Cancer Center	We shall be the premier cancer center in the world, based on the excellence of our people, our research-driven patient care and our science.
Massachusetts General Hospital	To seek ways to deliver the highest quality health care to all
Tampa General Hospital	To be the safest and most innovative academic health system in America
AdventHealth Hospital	Wholistic care to help you feel whole. Exceptional care at every step. Connecting you to the care you need. Dedicated to delivering access to affordable care. Innovative, viable care that adapts to your needs.

> **SELF-EXAM**
>
> Consider your organization's vision statement. How might you reword it to be most relevant for your functional team?

Values: "How We Live"

Typically, your espoused values declare what you stand for and how you work. Values can be either high-level, philosophical values or operational-level values that guide behaviors and day-to-day decisions.

Table 5-3. Values Examples

Organization	Values	
Mayo Clinic	▪ Respect ▪ Integrity ▪ Compassion ▪ Healing	▪ Teamwork ▪ Innovation ▪ Excellence ▪ Stewardship
St. Jude Children's Research Hospital	▪ Compassion ▪ Unity	▪ Equality ▪ Inclusion
Cleveland Clinic	▪ Quality and safety ▪ Empathy ▪ Inclusion	▪ Integrity ▪ Teamwork ▪ Innovation
University of Texas MD Anderson Cancer Center	▪ Caring ▪ Integrity	▪ Discovery
Massachusetts General Hospital	▪ Social, economic, and racial justice ▪ Healthcare as a human right ▪ Diversity	▪ Inclusion ▪ Education for all ▪ Equity ▪ Partnership and collaboration
Tampa General Hospital	▪ Integrity ▪ Compassion ▪ Accountability	▪ Excellence ▪ Courage
AdventHealth Hospital	▪ Quality and service excellence ▪ Community well-being ▪ High ethical standards	▪ Stewardship ▪ Inclusiveness
	Operational: 1. Keep me safe. 2. Love me. 3. Make it simple. 4. Own the problem.	

SELF-EXAM

Consider your organization's values. How might you reword them to be most relevant for your functional team?

Re-Envisioning Your Non-Negotiables

The emphasis of this book is implementation, but it's important to establish your current situation before trying to determine any gap. Ask yourself (and later, your team members) the following to orient this first step:

- What are the most significant values among your team (not necessarily those espoused by your organization)?
- What behaviors or physical evidence would an outsider notice that indicates your values?
- What behaviors or physical evidence would indicate they are not truly valued?
- What strengths or weaknesses are a result of these insights? How do they help or hurt your efforts to improve?

Now, before we go too much further down this road, it's important to bring up a contrarian view of the whole mission-vision-values situation:

As mere statements, they don't change anything!

But please bear with me—and this critical process. These statements are still important as a *starting* place for your team's success.

Virtually all big organizations who have failed have had mission statements, vision statements, and values—in nice, tidy packages. For example, the values of respect, integrity, communication, and excellence sound good, don't they?

They were the values of the infamous (and extinct) Enron Corporation—guilty of the biggest ($74 billion) accounting-fraud conspiracies in U.S. history. (Ouch!)

The takeaway is this: Establishing philosophical values and so on by itself doesn't accomplish anything. They merely allow for a more practical discussion about:

- What behaviors best bring those values to life in our unique function?
- How can we deliver those behaviors to consistently exceed the expectations of those we serve?

This is where you and your team can start developing your own tools to start your breakthrough.

The purpose for investing time and effort into establishing effective non-negotiables is so they can serve as an operational tool. A tool that dramatically improves decision making, productivity, and nearly every other aspect of the organization's existence. This applies to your team level as well. It's not overstating to say that a well-designed mission, vision, and values, when integrated into all aspects of the operation, make everything easier and better.

Everything.

"A vision without a task is but a dream. A task without a vision is drudgery. A vision and a task are the hope of the world."

— Inscription on a church wall in Sussex, England, c. 1730

The real challenge is getting your vision off the wall and into your—and your team's—daily behaviors. Margaret Mead once famously said, "Never doubt that a small group of thoughtful, committed citizens can change the world. Indeed, it is the only thing that ever has." Your role as the leader of this effort is to generate buy-in, ownership, and passion from your team. The best way to accomplish this is to optimize involvement from the members of your team. In his classic book *The Fifth Discipline*, Peter Senge shares a helpful five-stage model of this process when working with your team to develop a mission, vision, or values—evolving from most directive/least engaging to least directive/most engaging.[22]

- **Stage One: Telling—**Stating "I know what the mission/vision/values are. We've got to do this so adopt them or else." Obviously,

[22] Senge, 2006.

this approach is not very effective for generating true buy-in. They may follow along, but their primary motivation will likely be mere compliance. And then, only while you are actively watching them.

- **Stage Two: Selling**—Attempting to enroll people by stating "I have the best answer; let's see if I can convince you to go along" isn't very effective, either. Unless the team says yes wholeheartedly, this approach will fall short on real commitment.
- **Stage Three: Testing**—This is where you offer a "straw horse" version of the mission, vision, or values and introduce it as a starting point for discussion. This can be a helpful place to begin if your team is not as forthcoming as they could be. Laying the draft out for testing can generate some helpful feedback, but too often results in silent disagreement by some of the team. One way to improve the results of this approach is to engage team members individually first, so they can share their thoughts about what aspects are useful and not, before presenting the draft to the entire team.
- **Stage Four: Consulting**—This approach starts with "I want to develop a team mission/vision/set of values to help us better align our efforts and get better results, but I want to start with learning your collective thoughts." If you feel your team is relatively cooperative, then you may be able to start at this stage. You can begin by sharing different examples and asking which ones they would be willing to adopt or adapt. This can be a helpful stage if you don't have a trained facilitator.
- **Stage Five: Co-creating**—Approaching your team with an opportunity to develop a fully customized mission/vision/values set is the ultimate stage in fully collaborating and involving each member of your team. While you may opt to begin by reviewing various examples like those provided in this book, you can choose to simply clarify the intent of a mission statement, a vision statement, or team values in alignment with your organization (for operational integrity) and facilitate your

team in creating them together. I've found that this process, while a bit more meandering than earlier stages, can result in effective alignment tools and valuable team building. Building something together that is important and benefits everyone is a fantastic motivator. Knowing that you accomplished it together creates a camaraderie that is difficult to replicate otherwise.

With this in mind, a great place to start this process is by obtaining your existing organizational mission, vision, and values. Use them as a reference to begin crafting your own team version. For your team non-negotiables to be effective, they must be aligned with your higher-level organizational statements—just reworded to reflect your unique team function and the behaviors required to successfully deliver your daily responsibilities in a way that consistently exceeds the expectations of those in your care. Table 5-4 is a worksheet to develop your thoughts.

Table 5-4. Operational Non-Negotiables Worksheet

Our Organizational Vision:					
Our Organizational Purpose or Mission:					
Fully Aligned and Customized Team Versions					
Our Team Vision:					
Our Team Purpose or Mission:					
Values	1.	2.	3.	4.	5.
Value Definition					
Team Standards					
Tangible Team Behavior	1.	1.	1.	1.	1.
	2.	2.	2.	2.	2.
	3.	3.	3.	3.	3.

If you find that your organizational values are too unwieldy (or nonexistent), I recommend the following as a place to start creating your operational values. This tool has been an extraordinary help by providing a decision-making guide that unifies behaviors across teams.

This is a two-step process:

1. Select three to five operational values.
2. Prioritize them so they can also be used as a decision-making tool.

Starting with Disney's operational values, you can see how the equivalent healthcare version could be in Table 5-5.

Table 5-5. Comparing Disney and Healthcare Values

	Disney Value	Healthcare Value	Healthcare-Priority Rationale
1	Safety	Safety	Patients assume this is 100 percent: physical and emotional safety.
2	Courtesy	Compassion	Patients can't gauge the clinical aspects, but they can always determine if they've been treated well.
3	Show ("Image")	Professional	Subpar professionalism during any part of the experience undermines credibility—and confidence in the care.
4	Efficiency	Efficiency	Yes, patients want efficiency, but not at the expense of any of the other values.

The way this works in a healthcare decision-making scenario is as follows.

If an incident occurs and something needs to happen, the first question should be: "Is this situation appropriately safe for those involved?" If not, stop there and ensure that the situation is sufficiently safe.

If the safety situation is fine, then go to the next standard, compassion, and ask yourself: "Is this situation appropriately compassionate to those I'm serving?" If not, stop and improve it.

If the compassion is acceptable, go on to the third value and ask: "Is this situation a professional reflection on my healthcare organization?" If not, stop and make it better.

If the professionalism is fine, go to the fourth operational value, which is: "Is this situation as efficient as it could be?" And we can almost always find ways to make things more efficient.

As a quick aside, when considering these questions, we must acknowledge that nothing in this life is 100 percent, so this is not demanding perfection, merely that we meet or exceed our "higher than expected" standards of excellence. When I was in EMS/Fire Rescue, for example, we were never on an accident scene that was 100 percent safe, but we used *appropriate* safety tools and procedures to mitigate those risks to an acceptable level in order to save lives.

This prioritization process reflects what is most important to those in your care, whether they are patients (and their families), external operational partners, or internal colleagues. Keep in mind that *they* decide whether they are satisfied and what they will tell their family and friends about the experience. The way we engage them will affect their attitude while they are receiving care, as well as their intent to return or refer.

We can all agree that patient safety must be of utmost concern. Quite frankly, because of current industry efforts, more than 99.9 percent of the time, that is not the biggest gap for organizations (of course, we must continue to improve in any way possible). With enough focus, almost any organization can get safety right. Even a mediocre organization can rate well on one of these four values, perhaps even two or three, but only the best organizations manage to excel at all four. The difference is that world-class organizations can get safety right *without* sacrificing compassion, professionalism, or efficiency. An extraordinary healthcare experience consistently delivers all values that are important to your patients. That determines their choice of who gets their healthcare business.

Triaging Your Non-Negotiables

The healthcare industry is swirling with a wide variety of significant issues—safety, technology, pharma, political, community, legal, financial. Having a well-thought-out collection of concepts to keep these competing demands properly balanced is a critical skill. You have to keep in mind the most important reason your organization exists: To provide healthcare for those in need.

Many large corporations face similar issues, and it's interesting to see what the most successful organizations choose to prioritize. Take Amazon founder and CEO Jeff Bezos, who publishes an annual letter for his stakeholders. In it, he frequently refers to the five principles that he believes are the north star for their tech company:[23]

[23] Mullaney, 2017.

"1. Obsess over customers, not competitors... 2. Take risks for market leadership... 3. Make employees think like owners... 4. Build a culture that's right for your company... 5. Empower people."

Here's the big takeaway: Notice that, of the many things Bezos feels are important, he narrows it down to five (focus and simplicity make powerful tools). Of those five, Amazon, a tech company that operates almost solely in a virtual world, emphasizes *people* in four of the five, and includes a principle for risk and leadership. Even an Amazon new hire who started this morning can grasp that, to be successful at Amazon, they must prioritize people, growth, and progress. Simple and powerful in a complex organization of more than 750,000 employees!

While no organization is perfect, my personal litmus test for whether an organization or team is successful is when you hear outsiders characterize the company's branded behaviors as "That's so (fill in the name of the company)". I would often hear people say at Disney, "Gee, only at Disney would something like that (good experience aligned with the brand) happen!" One example that Fred Lee mentioned in *If Disney Ran Your Hospital* was the expectation that cast members (Disney employees) would pick up trash. Because cleanliness was determined to be an industry differentiator, Disney makes sure that everyone is trained—and held accountable—for behaviors that exhibit their commitment to keeping the parks and resorts clean for their guests.

This operational integrity between intent and behaviors is a key component to creating a strong identity and reputation. In times of adversity, having a dependable reputation can positively influence your interactions with staff and patients alike.

As Fred made clear in his book, one of the key ways that your hospital is different from Disney is the depth of the interactions you have with patients, and I couldn't agree more. Many people who come to a hospital or similar healthcare organization for clinical care are *far* more vulnerable than they would typically be at a hotel, retail store, or theme park. Mere courtesy, while nice in a hospitality industry setting, is *wholly insufficient* in your healthcare environment. Anyone who claims otherwise is suspect, in my opinion.

As you develop your team's values, I want to strongly encourage you to consider the following: For many years, it has been common practice for healthcare organizations to encourage healthcare professionals to embrace *empathy* (the ability to understand and share the feelings of another) when dealing with patients and their families. This is done to establish a personal connection between caregiver and patient. As noble and well intentioned as that is, we have seen ever-increasing cases of burnout across all medical-care functions. Numerous studies have indicated that burnout has been fed by this practice of sharing the painful feelings that patients experience. Based on my involvement with numerous leading hospitals and medical centers around the world, the more appropriate value for healthcare is *compassion.*

Recently, Jeff Weiner, the CEO of LinkedIn, tweeted his thoughts about the importance of compassion: "Big misconception about managing compassionately is that it's a 'soft' skill. Most compassionate people I know are typically the strongest."[24]

Later, he published a LinkedIn blog post that went into more detail about the difference between compassion and empathy—and the importance of the more useful skill of compassion:

> As the Dalai Lama explains, if you are walking along a trail and come along a person who is being crushed by a boulder, an empathetic reaction would result in you feeling the same sense of crushing suffocation and render you unable to help. The compassionate reaction would put you in the sufferer's shoes, thinking this person must be experiencing horrible pain so you're going to do everything in your power to remove the boulder and alleviate their suffering. Put another way, compassion is a more objective form of empathy. This idea of seeing things clearly through another person's perspective can be invaluable when it comes to relating with others, particularly intense work situations.

---

[24] Weiner, 2017.

Where Magic Is Happening in Healthcare: Encompass Health

Encompass Health is the largest owner and operator of rehabilitation hospitals in the United States, to include 161 hospitals in 37 states and Puerto Rico. The company has developed a sterling reputation for providing high-quality, compassionate rehabilitative care for patients recovering from a major injury or illness, using advanced technology and innovative treatments to maximize recovery. Encompass Health has been ranked as one of *Fortune's World's Most Admired Companies* and *Modern Healthcare's Best Places to Work* in *Healthcare* the past four years in a row.

This impressive growth comes from operationally reinforcing "The Encompass Health Way" values of: Set The Standard, Lead With Empathy, Do What's Right, Focus On The Positive, and Stronger Together" with a regular implementation accountability effort. All functional teams, clinical and non-clinical, discuss patient care daily with direct links to those guiding values. Keeping their core non-negotiables "front of mind" is the criteria that leads to behaviors that are "front and center" to the staff and patient experiences.

This emphasis on consistency and integrity between their values and their actions has caught the attention of local hospitals who seek to refer to partner operations that will earn not just an extraordinary patient experience, but superior clinical outcomes as well. Encompass Health has earned a reputation for taking on more complicated cases such as stroke patients, and brain/spinal cord injuries and having an extremely low occurrence of those challenging patients being readmitted to the hospital. Encompass team members create values-based experiences that earn accolades, then local hospitals and physicians respond by directing patients to Encompass facilities, which feeds organic growth and success — all from committing to using their values as operational tools.

When using these new tools to focus your team's efforts and resources, there will be some trial and error as part of this natural process. Managing new ideas requires some clarity about what is a viable, appropriate option and what is not.

Now that we've established what tools world-class organizations create to most effectively align efforts to create extraordinary experiences, let's continue with more details about how to ensure those experiences are everything you want them to be.

6

Creating Team Magic in Your Real World

"The keynote of progress ... is system and organization— in other words, 'team work.'"

— Charles H. Mayo

Regardless of a healthcare professional's individual skills, the fact remains that every patient is cared for, directly or indirectly, by numerous people in the organization. Patient care is a team activity. So, the ability to work well with others in delivering quality care is always a vital part of your team's and organization's culture.

What Makes an Extraordinary Team?

When my team was working with Google, they had just completed a deep-dive study about what characteristics reflected the highest-performing teams, called Project Aristotle (named after the philosopher's famous quote that "the whole is greater than the sum of its parts"). After a thorough analysis of 180 teams and hundreds of double-blind interviews, they discovered that the strongest correlations for high-performing team cultures is:

- **Meaning:** The work is personally meaningful to team members
- **Psychological safety:** A shared belief that the team is safe for personal risk taking
- **Structure and clarity:** The team's plans and goals are clearly understood
- **Dependability:** When teammates say they'll do something, they do it
- **Impact:** The work matters

The good news? You can influence every single one of these characteristics! Great teams are built on the foundation of trust, collaboration, and commitment. Developing your team culture is the key!

SELF-EXAM:

How would you rate your team on each of these considerations? Consider these characteristics and how you can help improve them as you explore the tools throughout this book.

Do You Have a Culture of Care That Works?

You've likely heard about how important corporate culture is, particularly in helping increase engagement and results. I like to describe the culture as simply the personality of your team or organization. As researcher Denise Lee Yohn states in her book *Fusion: How Integrating Brand and Culture Powers the World's Greatest Companies*, "A company's culture doesn't need to be 'warm and fuzzy' to be effective ... The company succeeds because it has a single, unifying drive behind its internal culture and its external brand."[25] Your culture exists either by design or by default. The key question is: "Do you have the team culture that best serves your values and purpose?" If not, you have the opportunity—and responsibility—to change that.

Scott Rosenthal, CEO of NEOHealth, a federally qualified health system,

[25] Yohn, 2018.

ranks having a culture of patient-centricity as a priority—even on a budget:[26]

> The key is making [the] experience the best it can be. Patients have choices where they spend their medical dollar, so taking that seriously is a priority. Internal culture is everything. Disney says "Everything speaks," and it does: *How clean is the building; televisions in the waiting room; waiting room clean; lessen the wait time; get the patient scheduled when they want to be; after-hours options.* It's all driven by people. And attitude is everything. We have a couple of books assigned to all employees annually. At our meetings, we ask questions from the book, and anyone who answers the questions receives a prize. One idea they had was to give a Hershey Kiss to our patients when they leave. It's called "Our Kiss Goodbye" and meant to teach our employees to say thank you, and it works. Patients love it.

Mike Mahoney, CEO of Boston Scientific, one of MIT Sloan's top-20 culture companies and leading medical-device developers, states: "We're fortunate that in healthcare, we don't have to look far for our purpose—our mission is to transform lives. Our devices and therapies help more than 30 million patients each year. It's not a question of doing the right thing instead of focusing on the bottom line; it's about doing the right thing as the best way to achieve sustainable, long-term growth."[27] According to one employee, "The answer to every question for a project is 'making something better for the patient.'"[28]

Do you have the team culture that best serves your values and purpose?

This chapter will explore ways that you can guide your team's culture toward the most effective alignment among your values, your mission, and those you serve—and make your everyday outcomes better and easier to achieve in the long run.

---

[26] Rosenthal, 2018.

[27] Mahoney, 2020.

[28] Ibid.

As the team leader (or an aspiring team leader), you are expected to model the behaviors mentioned in these chapters as well. You set the tone. You set the expectations. You must lead the culture by modeling the way.

To optimize your team's results, you must first gain deeper engagement with your team and guide them toward better engagement with one another and those they care for. Any change—even if it will be an improvement—will be resisted unless you first establish a foundation of trust and credibility with your team.

Engage in Being Engaging

You've certainly gotten the requests to increase engagement—both among your team as well as with the patients. Engagement is just another way to say, "Connect with them to create better interactions and outcomes." In any people-focused business, healthy engagement is the cornerstone of world-class results.

Typically, engagement surveys include questions such as:

- How clear are you on the expectations for you in your role?
- How meaningful is your work?
- How well do you and your team take care of each other?
- How good is the quality of work that you and your team do?
- How often do you receive feedback or praise regarding your efforts?

In fact, Gallup found that in 2023, only 33 percent of employees were fully engaged, with the lack of engagement leading to "about $1.9 trillion in lost productivity."[29]

In 2020, Gallup found that "team members with higher levels of engagement:

- produce substantially better outcomes
- treat customers better and attract new ones
- are more likely to remain with their organization than those who are less engaged

---

[29] Harter, 2024.

Engaged employees are also healthier and less likely to experience burnout."[30]

Obviously, the goal is to optimize engagement. But how? Let's begin exploring tools to transform your culture by recalibrating your team's relationships and results.

Recalibrating Team Relationships

A primary cause of team anxiety and subpar performance is a lack of clarity regarding their leader's expectations. Fortunately, you are in complete control of your efforts to resolve this. A great place to begin is to make sure everyone on your team understands where you are coming from as the team leader. When starting with a new team, a best practice is to write up a "let's get to know each other" orientation letter prior to the first meeting to guide discussion. If you are recalibrating an existing team, you can simply use the letter as talking points in your next meeting.

Include information such as the following:

- Context setting: Establish your desire to make a difference as a unified team, which requires understanding one another.
- What you must all agree on: Your organization's core non-negotiables should be the measuring stick of every decision, in order to exceed the expectations of those you serve—both patients and colleagues.
- You expect every person to contribute to the best of their ability to building and maintaining healthy workplace relationships and superior results—in other words, to being a benchmark team.
- What matters to you, your preferences, and your pet peeves (such as how you prefer communication).
- Your strengths and the traits you are working to improve.
- You expect them to improve every aspect of their work to make the biggest difference to patients, the team, and the organization.

---

[30] Harter, 2020.

- You are committed to supporting them through the process that you all share.
- Remind them they are role models. Their behaviors matter. They are always "onstage."
- Any final inspirational thoughts or quotes that mean something to you and why, in the hopes that they are motivational to your team as well.

"Hard work is a prison sentence only if it does not have meaning."

— Malcolm Gladwell

Start the Journey Together

Every successful transformation starts with the team acknowledging that things need to be better. More important, they need to agree that there is hope that it *can* be better and be motivated to start that journey together. This is a four-step discussion.

Step One: The first part of this book details how healthcare is being disrupted. This is obvious to everyone on your team, but it can help if you can provide some evidence-based data that clearly show trends and patterns in the healthcare industry. In addition to the content from this book, uncover some relevant details that directly pertain to your function or organization. Goal: Gain agreement that the team is not where you all want to be.

Step Two: Continue the discussion with each teammate's desire or healthcare calling—what kind of day-to-day experience they would have and what experiences would they give patients or those they serve. Goal: Showcase how compelling that goal is and the gap between where you are now and where you all want to be as a team.

Step Three: Introduce the fact that there are organizations in healthcare (or you can compare other teams in your hospital) that are thriving amid the same circumstances your organization or team is experiencing. Despite having similar resources, they are getting better results because how they are using the resources is superior to what you are doing. Goal: Create hope that the team can bridge the gap to what matters most to them by following proven strategies and tools (that you happen to have access to in this book!)

Step Four: Finally, discuss how you can begin developing and implementing these tools and making progress that helps you influence your circumstances. Goal: Commit to making consistent progress, following the approach of world-class organizations to improve the team's work experience, their patient experiences, and ultimate outcomes ... and bring to life the reason they went into healthcare as a profession.

Keep in mind that the commitment process for any team member will happen in different ways at different times in this process. Table 6-1 has some milestones to look for.

Table 6-1. Commitment Milestones

Stage:	**Aware**	**Understand**	**Buy-In**	**Ownership**	**Advocate**
Look For:	"I've heard of it."	"I know what it is."	"I agree with it and do it."	"I'm implementing it consistently."	"I lead it and tell everyone the benefits."

Everyone's perspective of their progress (including yours) will be at different places because they were possibly introduced to the initiative at different times, and have a different speed to digest, get comfortable with, and begin trying out new behaviors. Your goal is to support each team member in the unique circumstances that they are in at each stage of their development.

The following graph (Figure 6-1) shows an example of how your team can develop through these milestones differently due to when you/they become aware and how they process the experience, assuming you introduce them to your intent one month after going through this book. Keep this mind to minimize your (and their) frustration.

Figure 6-1. Example of Team Commitment Development

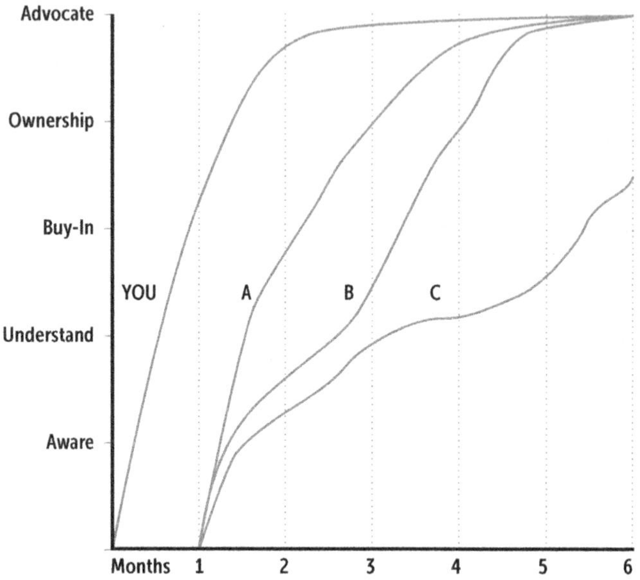

Common Obstacles to Team Commitment

Besides "getting them involved in creating the solution" to create buy-in, there are often specific difficulties team members can face when confronting efforts to change. The following obstacles are some common examples, with tips about how to overcome them.[31]

- Feeling there are no alternatives: Sometimes, when someone has fought against "the machine" for long enough, they give up and stop trying to improve things. Test everything you do to determine whether there is a better way. Try asking the following questions to get started:
    - When have people made exceptions to these processes or norms in the past?
    - Are we willing to try something different if it can align with our non-negotiables and better outcomes?

[31] Quinn et al., 2024, 56–9.

    - What other organizations have successfully handled similar situations differently? How?
- Feeling there is no hope: When people have been struggling in an unrelenting environment for a significant length of time (sound familiar?), it is human nature to begin losing hope that things can be different. It doesn't take too many failed change initiatives to resign someone to an attitude of "just tell me what to do." To encourage someone to try again, consider the following:
    - Review past successes: Look at the details of what created breakthroughs in those scenarios and look for ways to apply those ideas to this situation.
    - Involve others: Seeking out different viewpoints can often unlock new thinking about how to solve the problem. The newest people on the team often have a fresh perspective.
    - Break down the larger action items into smaller, more manageable tasks: This can keep the challenge from being too overwhelming and encourage your team to take that first intimidating step.
- Feeling there is no time: The healthcare industry, particularly urgent care, is often working at nonstop breakneck speeds. You may be understaffed, and everything is urgent, but there are options that can provide some relief:
    - How could you improve organizational inefficiencies? Often the solution to reducing the demands on our time is to innovate more efficient solutions. Not only can this reduce the pressure you are enduring, but it can free up time to invest in more strategic activities, like self-care! (The next chapter has a helpful time-management tool that has proven very effective for this!)
    - How can we surface and address conflict? The biggest time suck is dealing with conflict that has not yet been managed properly. It is human nature to avoid conflict, so dealing with it effectively is rare and often difficult, because people

aren't experienced at addressing it. (There is a tool to address conflict and accountability near the end of this chapter to help you with this specific challenge.)

Once the team has a general willingness to make the effort to improve, begin the action of co-creating your team's exciting new chapter.

> **PRO TIP**
>
> One of the best no-cost ways I've found to improve my team culture is to simply ask each member, "How can I help you get better results from your on-the-job efforts?" and actively listen. Then take appropriate action. Then let them know you acted on their feedback because it, and they, matter. Repeat.

Aligning You and Your Team

An effective alignment tool used to guide teams and team leaders through a series of topics that don't come up often in workplace conversation is to share responses to strategic team issues. To ensure that all members of the team can share their opinions on each issue, distribute them and explain the purpose of the activity (to gather their best insights), then discuss opinions and solutions at the next meeting. This tool gives both the leader and the team a chance to share their concerns about preferred interaction styles, to discuss how the team can more effectively work together, and to clarify expected results—dramatically shortening the time it takes for a group to become a more productive team.

I've led or been part of dozens of these exercises, and it invariably results in team members learning a lot about one another—leading to better understanding and improved clarity of efforts *much* more quickly and efficiently. Some sample questions include:

- What are your expectations for the coming year?
- What would top performance look like on our team?

- What are your strengths?
- How do you prefer getting communication? Example: Big picture versus details first?
- How do you prefer to receive feedback?
- What is your preferred way to manage conflict?
- What are your weaknesses or areas for improvement?
- What are this team's biggest opportunities for improvement?
- What are our biggest challenges to achieving our goals?

The team leader and team members each complete the questions (download the full document at **ResultsStat.com/BookResources**.) Essentially, each person has the same questions, focusing on their perspective. Here's the overall process that seems to work best:

1. The leader and team members work individually to:
   - Provide information they want to share with the group about themselves (enhancing relationships)
   - Develop questions they want to ask the group to understand their preferred work styles (enhancing results)
2. After sharing preferences and developing a list of improvement opportunities, both the leader and the team members prioritize their lists based on perceived importance and the amount of time and effort required to accomplish them.
3. The leader and team meet to systematically discuss identified issues, striving to better understand one another and explore options to optimize their performance as a unified team.

The discussions from this activity can be so rich that teams often need more than one session to finish. The results usually include resolution to misunderstandings, a better appreciation for one another, and increased confidence about moving toward shared goals.

Relieving Burnout by Restoring Balance

One significant consideration for getting anyone to support a new effort to improve your team results is to acknowledge the timing—and address supporting them in their struggle with being overwhelmed by all the recent demands on them. For some, particularly in healthcare, that includes experiencing burnout.

No human being can be subjected to a pandemic (or any similarly harrowing scenario) and escape without being affected by stress. The January–February 2024 *Harvard Business Review* had an article about how to sustain compassion in difficult times that articulated recent healthcare experiences brilliantly: "In emergency and critical-care settings, physicians, nurses, and social workers encounter a stream of people who are having the worst day of their lives. These workers drink from a firehose of human misery, go home to care for their own families, and then return to do it all over again."[32] Given that anyone's passion for healthcare will be undermined if they're not operating at their best, it is vital to prioritize self-care.

PRO TIP

When your team experiences you prioritizing their health, it will likely lead to new levels of trust, communication, and support. Always a fantastic investment of your efforts!

Healthcare can be an incredibly intense and draining experience—even on the best of days. You're dealing with volatile scenarios and a wide range of human emotions, but it's important to recognize the difference between being overwhelmed, which is temporary, and being legitimately burned out and in need of professional support. "Burnout can undermine not only employee well-being, but also patient outcomes, safety and quality of care. Employees who feel burnout are three times more likely to leave and 63% more likely to take a sick day. For organizations, burnout translates to increased turnover, lost productivity and increased malpractice lawsuits," according to a 2018 Gallup article.[33]

---

[32] Zaki, 2024.

[33] Plemmons, 2018.

The Mayo Clinic has a helpful guide called "Job Burnout: How to Spot It and Take Action" that provides some guidance on identifying symptoms. Here is a sample of the questions:

- Do you have to drag yourself to work and have trouble getting started once you arrive?
- Do you lack the energy to be consistently productive?
- Are you using food, drugs, or alcohol to feel better or to simply not feel anything?
- Have your sleep habits or appetite changed?
- Are you troubled by unexplained headaches, backaches, or other physical ailments?

While I'm a deeply committed proponent of developing individual resilience and agility, there are valid times for seeking help. That said, if the issue is more a temporary phase of being overwhelmed, you can work to zero in on what is causing the problem. Table 6-2 has some examples and possible solutions to help relieve the situation.

Table 6-2. Overwhelm Causes and Solutions

Cause	Solutions to Consider
Lack of Control	Let go of issues outside your control, or develop your influence to expand your ability to better manage those issues currently out of reach.
Poor Job Fit	Determine the abilities required for success in your position, then either build capabilities or seek out a new role that better fits your interests.
Dysfunctional Workplace Dynamics	Identify disrupters among your team and lead the effort to improve the dynamics to everyone's benefit.
Overwhelmed With Tasks	Get more efficient at completing tasks, or prioritize your obligations by importance and delete or delegate whatever you don't have time to do in partnership with your leader(s).
Lack of Social Support	If you feel isolated, make the effort to engage with colleagues and build a supportive relationship network.
Work-Life Imbalance	Examine your time, energy, and resources, then prioritize, organize, and let go of whatever you need to for better "balance" (it will never be perfect).

[34] Mayo Clinic Staff, 2023.

The "time, energy, and resources" aspect of this last point is a critical issue to resolve. One tool to begin this journey is to identify ways to better manage your finite energy (the time and resources aspects will get covered in the next chapter).

You and your team can benefit from valuable insights by clearly identifying what drains you of energy and what refreshes your energy levels. High-performing teams use guides like Table 6-3 to organize their inner thoughts and external issues to begin improving options—minimizing what drains and maximizing what energizes.

Table 6-3. Improving What Drains or Energizes You

What Drains Me	Inner Improvements	External Improvements
What Energizes Me	**Inner Improvements**	**External Improvements**

Tool Tips

Step One: Make a list of your work activities and how they affect your energy level. This is typically easier if every team member does this first individually.

For most people, it's easier to start with what drains them. List the activities that chew up your energy, then consider:

- What you can do emotionally or mentally (inner improvements) to better deal with that draining task. Why is it, specifically, so bothersome? What makes you so impatient with the task? Will getting better at the task make it less draining for you? Might an attitude change improve this situation? What boundaries can you create to help you stay energized?

- What you can do with the external dynamics—the things or people involved—to decrease the way it affects your energy level.

Step Two: List what energizes you, then fill out improvement considerations—how to increase the opportunities to engage in these activities, both internally and externally.

Step Three: Share insights among the team. I recommend starting with what energizes each team member, perhaps limiting it to their most energizing work activity. Next, have each person share the one work activity that drains them the most. After each person shares their task-drain insights, ask for encouraging tips from the other team members. Some questions to ask the team can include:

- Who else is drained by this? (Most feel better if they aren't the only one feeling the drain.)
- Who here isn't drained by this task? What is your secret?
- What can we do to make this task easier? Is it possible to delete this task somehow?

Finally, take team notes and ask everyone to work together to help support everyone's personal improvement effort. It is important to set your team up for success by helping them prepare for the team improvement effort that is to come.

Recalibrating Results

After you work with your team to relieve some pressure from their immediate challenges (and deepen much-needed relationships), they will be better prepared to begin recalibrating how they achieve results. The first step will be to get everyone involved in addressing your primary tool for navigating change to ensure improvements: Your core non-negotiables.

Team Tool: Team Non-Negotiables

Building off the initial content and individual work you did in Chapter 4, provide the team-focused worksheets to your team, explaining the purpose of generating guidance that is more relevant for your functional roles.

Follow the same process you did when completing your own thoughts for developing your team's version of the mission, vision, and values—adapted to be most relevant to your unique function.

1. Review your organization's mission statement. What implication does it have regarding why your team exists? Which aspects are most relevant to your operation? How might you distill the larger mission to what you do every day?
2. Review your organization's vision statement. How does your team's function support where you are going as a larger organization? What team version of the vision could capture your aspirational goal for a compelling future?
3. Review your organization's values. How is each value relevant to your day-to-day team function? How does each value affect those you serve? What behaviors best bring each value to life in your specific situation?

Once you and your team clarify the (typically) philosophical mission, vision, and values into more practical, team-related tools, document your team's collective finished products by posting them where they can be referenced throughout your workday. Help keep their core non-negotiables top of mind by connecting to them as you discuss daily behaviors and outcomes.

Team Tool: Continue-Stop-Start

This next activity doesn't require any materials other than chart paper or a whiteboard. But don't let the simplicity of this fool you into thinking it isn't a powerful, game-changing experience for your team.

The purpose is to guide a discussion to identify what the team wants to improve. Many teams fumble through these kinds of discussions, but there is a strategic approach that makes your outcomes much more effective, called "Continue-Stop-Start."

As we've discussed, it's human nature to resist change to some extent. To make matters worse, most change initiatives make the huge mistake of completely changing an approach to work, usually because some consulting firm wants to license a "soup-to-nuts system" that inexplicably denies the effective efforts the team or organization is currently doing. This leads to the workforce being demoralized (all their hard work for nothing) and disconnected (because the leader has lost credibility, and they give up).

Foolish on SO many levels! Yes, one of my (many) pet peeves.

A *much* better solution is to identify what is working well and build off that by removing ineffective actions and beginning new, more effective actions.

Start by recognizing that their efforts have earned success in a significant part of their work—knowing that the moment someone comments that they want to change something, there is likely to be pushback. Inoculate the team against this problem by directly involving them in identifying what will *not* change.

Mention that this activity has two parts—making a list, then brainstorming solutions. Begin the activity by asking:

1. What do you think is working well that we should *continue* doing for now?

Starting with this question helps people who are nervous about any change to relax and be more open to supporting the needed improvement efforts. This also ensures that you will not change something that already works well enough for now, which helps provide a measure of stability as well as give your team the opportunity to be involved in the process - which leads to improved buy-in, ownership, and passion about supporting the change effort. Record their thoughts for all to see and identify any strong disagreements regarding significant issues. Note those topics for future discussion. Then, shift to the next question:

2. What do you think is not working for us and we should *stop* doing?

This question strategically provides an opportunity for people to identify the things that don't make sense, are frustrating, and waste their time and energy. Record the things the team is currently doing that no longer serve your patient or staff experience. This often generates quite a bit of energy and can lead to a long list. Once finished, mention that this list will be referenced later. Then, ask the third and final question of this activity:

3. What do you think we should *start* doing that would add value and help achieve the aspirations discussed in earlier team activities?

Brainstorm a list of things that you could begin doing to add value to the patient experience, while not negatively affecting the staff experience or the operational or financial situation. Record their answers. Acknowledge that the stop and start lists will become action items for improvement efforts moving forward. Also remind them that these lists are living documents that can be added to and changed as directed by the team. As mentioned earlier, an important element of this process is to engage and involve everyone throughout. This is what creates buy-in and ownership of your team-improvement project.

Finally, note that this discussion is a good start, but that implementing their ideas will be what brings them to life. If at all possible, begin work immediately on brainstorming low- and no-cost solutions. Commit to working together to leverage your collective insights, resources (including people who can help with certain plans), and influence for not just these list items, but also growing toward a larger, more strategic goal in alignment with your team's non-negotiables. Before you wrap up, ask yourself, how will you best support the team's efforts in implementing these ideas? How can you best support one another?

Vital Behaviors for Team Excellence

Every functional team requires particular skills. To optimize your team potential, it is important that you collectively identify which behaviors matter most to your mutual success.

One way that I like to start this team process is to brainstorm feedback you've received about particularly helpful behaviors that led to exceeding expectations. These comments can be from patients about their caregivers or from staff (both within and outside this team) who have provided insights about helpful behaviors. This list typically reveals trends of similar descriptors that you can organize into different traits, such as compassionate, respectful, and informative.

Once you have these important traits identified, you'll be able to start using this information by translating it into the specific behaviors required to bring the traits to life in your day-to-day operation. One way to guide this discussion is to use Table 6-4, which includes a few examples.

Table 6-4. Identifying Vital Team Skills

Desired Trait	Impact on Experience (Feedback)	Behaviors	Role model
Compassionate	"They obviously cared about the fear I had and communicated that everything would be all right."	▪ Direct eye contact ▪ Hand on shoulder ▪ Soft tone of voice ▪ Encouraging words ▪ Followed up	Emma
Respectful	"They took my symptoms seriously and made sure to record all my concerns."	▪ Direct eye contact ▪ Asked clarifying questions ▪ Referred to me as "Sir"	Ellen
Informative	"I didn't have to wait to get updated. They initiated the conversation, walking me through all the confusing information until I was clear about next treatment steps."	▪ Direct eye contact ▪ Shared difficult info quickly and clearly ▪ Was very detailed ▪ Answered all my questions ▪ Provided contact info	Frank

Once you have clarified the specific behaviors that create the desired traits, you can begin the process of helping everyone on your team develop their skills for optimal success.

PRO TIP

One solution is to identify the person on your team (or, if needed, someone whom your team has access to) who already consistently delivers the targeted behavior(s). Ask them for any tips they can provide to generate the outcomes your team is looking for. Follow up regularly with your team for the first few weeks to help keep this development effort top of mind. [See next team tool.]

Team Tool: Skills Audit and Enhancement

Next, as a related way to tap into the valuable resources you already have, implement a team skills audit. This audit activity is a staple of many team-improvement efforts, and includes the following:

1. Brainstorm with your team the specific skills needed to be successful in your team's operational mission.
2. Prioritize the list so the most vital skills are on top.
3. Have the team identify the one to three members of your team who are the best at each of the vital skills at the top of your list. (You can complete the list as you make progress, but start with the skills most necessary for team success.)
4. Enlist each person best at their skill to share tips on what they do differently and better to achieve superior results.
5. Arrange a way to disseminate the helpful tips and schedule accordingly.

Table 6-5 is an example of the worksheet.

Table 6-5. Team Skills Audit Worksheet

Priority	Skills Needed	Top Performers	Best Way to Share	Schedule Delivery

Work your way down the list and support each team member in improving their skills until you have a team full of superior performers. Not only does this low-cost approach develop each member of your team in the skills most relevant to your mission success, but (bonus!) it typically generates greater engagement and teamwork, which enhances your team culture.

Team Tool: Filling Team Gaps

As you collectively work to develop optimal team capabilities, you want to leverage every advantage you have—some of which already exist among your team. One tool popular among the most renowned organizations is called "Team Weaver."

This tool provides multiple benefits. Primarily, it identifies the needs and support options among the team itself. It also consistently opens up opportunities to discuss ways that each team member is interdependent and how, with minor effort, they can dramatically transform the team's dynamics.

The tool setup is simple: Create a matrix of all the names of your team along both the x and y axes (Table 6-6):

Table 6-6. Team Weaver Worksheet

Team Weaver Worksheet		Support I <u>NEED</u> from my colleagues											
		Ellen		Beth		Stacy		Janice		Frank		Emma	
		Need	Help	Need	Help	Need	Help	Need	Help	Need	Help	Need	Help
Support I can provide my colleague	Ellen												
	Beth												
	Stacy												
	Janice												
	Frank												
	Emma												

Each box of the tool is divided in two sections to make space to record two factors:

- Left side: What support do I need from other team members to produce my best outcomes?
- Right side: How can I best support my teammates to help them produce their best outcomes?

The left side of each shared box is for the team members at the top to write what support they would like from each of the other team members. This request could be either results-focused (such as "Please write on the dry-erase board more legibly so I can better read your handwriting") or relationship-focused (such as "I'd like to better understand your approach to teamwork"). The right side of each shared box is for the team member to describe how they will commit to helping that person's request for support.

There are at least two ways you can conduct this activity. If your team is well established and close-knit with minimal communication or relationship problems, you can perform this activity (Table 6-6) on a chart paper with sticky notes. This not only allows for individual insights but also provides a venue for a teamwide discussion.

Another way that is "safer" for less-cohesive teams is to make copies of the (Table 6-7) pairing tool, distribute a copy to each team member to fill out (Table 6-7), and have each one pair off with another for five minutes or so to discuss the requests two people at a time. Each person can then have a private discussion with each team member, and they can record needs and support one pair at a time. Depending on how healthy your team dynamics are, you can then gather everyone together later to discuss the activity as a group and explore how to proceed as a team.

Table 6-7. Sample Individual Pairing Worksheet

Team Weaver: Ellen				
	I Need	Colleague Support	Colleague Need	My Support
Beth				

Regardless of which approach you select, the benefits of this activity include the following:

- Operational gaps between each team member can be addressed for improved efficiencies and accountability.
- Relational gaps can be enhanced to create a foundation for improved awareness and camaraderie.
- These discussions often develop into conversations (and better understanding) of how they all can work most effectively together to become the highest-performing team.

PRO TIP

When it comes to supporting your team, in addition to any feedback you receive from this team activity, as a leader, I always like to augment this by asking your team members to answer this question: "I wish (your name) knew ..." or "I wish (your name) did ..." The discussions tend to be very enlightening. 10/10. Strongly recommend.

Agile Teams Live the Dream

With all the healthcare changes happening now, and in the future, it is more critical than ever for your team to become as agile as possible. Effective agility is a combination of the following traits:

Focused: When everyone on the team is paying attention to the same things with shared goals, there is much less wasted time and effort.

PRO TIP

Clarifying the core non-negotiables will allow you to identify more easily what is and is not worthy of your team's limited time and energy.

Flexible: Because our external circumstances and the individual capabilities of each team member are constantly changing, being able to adjust effectively helps minimize the emotional, mental, and functional challenges that come with change.

PRO TIP

Having sufficient stabilizing "anchors" (like the non-negotiables) and tools to optimize flexibility (like the mental-health and effective communication tools I discussed) will set the stage for improved flexibility when needed.

Fast: The healthcare work environment is often characterized by a constant sense of urgency to rapidly iterate the adjustments needed to maintain equilibrium in the patient and clinical team experience. Given that patients and their families are with you in less-than-ideal circumstances, there is persistent pressure to quickly make things better. Prepare to *anticipate* changes!

PRO TIP

Identify any predictable actions and develop templates or hacks to address them, such as stock email responses to common requests.

Plush Toy Wow: Part Two of Three

If you recall the story about the housekeeper who moved the toys around and wowed the family of Disney fanatics, let me share with you how we followed up to reinforce that extraordinary behavior. The general manager (GM) wanted to recognize Judi's efforts, so he made plans to surprise her during her team's pre-shift team meeting later that week. The GM told them about the guest letter and that those behaviors were exactly what he was looking for to create "the Disney Difference." He read the letter, and the whole team responded with a collective "Aww" and applause. He revealed that the extraordinary team member was Judi and awarded her with a "Mousecar," which is a small, gold-colored Mickey Mouse statue that is occasionally presented to cast members who go above and beyond to creatively exceed the expectations of a guest.

One thing that most world-class organizations have in common is that their leaders exhibit what I call "investment mentality" anytime they spend a penny of their budget or a minute of their time or effort. When the GM prepared how to best reinforce the plush-toy behavior, he purposefully planned to create multiple returns on investment. The first payoff was for Judi herself, who enjoyed getting noticed for her extra effort. She also appreciated the GM of the hotel making time to come express this in person, which was a benefit for the GM as well. An additional payoff is that the rest of the team was now trained on what kinds of behaviors will earn similar recognition and why they are important to Disney's reputation. The team also appreciated the leadership for making the effort—again, gaining valuable credibility and respect for the GM and the company. Finally, the experience motivated them to explore other creative, low- or no-cost ways to exceed expectations—even though they typically never interact with the guests they are assigned to. Everyone wins.

Establish Support Systems for Sustainability

Many people avoid saying nice things about their colleagues, thinking that it doesn't mean much. That may be true, *if* the comments are insincere or unearned. Even if people discount praise, they still know that you notice what they do, and appreciate their effort. When you link their behaviors to your team or company values or the impact they made on their patients, then team members also know that you share a common interest in making a difference to those you both care for.

Recognition and Rewards

Reinforce the new, improved behaviors by acknowledging those who contributed in a significant way. Make sure you recognize people for proactively managing situations, not just reacting to them. Encourage the effort to anticipate opportunities and avoid problems before they happen to discourage crisis management, which we all are sick of.

The first thing to consider is whether the behavior warrants acknowledgment (nothing kills the value of recognition more than undermining its meaning).

The most effective recognition is one that honors their effort and is something they care about or benefits those they care about. We've all witnessed the positive impact of sincere, well-delivered praise—and it is a powerful motivator that helps sustain any improvement effort.

This usually requires more than a vague "Good job," which doesn't make lasting impact. The following tool is a helpful template for crafting your own recognition that makes a difference:

1. Identify what they *specifically* did well.
2. Clarify how the behavior aligns with the mission, vision, or

values (and reflects integrity).

3. Share the benefit of the behavior to the patient, the team, or operational/financial interests.
4. Share that you *personally* appreciate their effort and look forward to more successes!

Accountability

Recognition and rewards aren't the only necessary tools to reinforce behaviors. Sometimes corrective actions are required to keep behaviors aligned with the non-negotiables and the rest of the team. Following the adage "Praise in public, criticize in private," any personal corrective discussions are best done away from others, to demonstrate mutual respect.

Hosting accountability discussions can be awkward at best and relationship-damaging (or even legal-action-inducing) at worst. The following popular GROW tool, developed by Sir John Whitmore in his book *Coaching for Performance*, can help make these discussions constructive and easier. This tool provides sequential guidance to navigate the discussion point by point. Typically, this tool is used to coach people to better align their efforts to achieve a team goal. Table 6-8 provides a quick overview.

Table 6-8. GROW Accountability Tool

Step	Description	Notes for Implementation
Goal	Ensure understanding of the shared goal.	
Reality	Objectively describe the current status.	
Options	Collaborate on solutions and improvements.	
Will You Do	Clarify action details and responsibilities.	

Prior to hosting an accountability discussion, prepare yourself with your best relationship-building communication. If you approach this opportunity skillfully, you can have this discussion to course-correct their behavior and build a more trusting relationship as well. Craft comments that avoid triggering an emotional reaction. Emphasize that your motivation for coaching them is so they can succeed in alignment with the rest of the team. Here is a simple process to get you ready to navigate this conversation:

1. Ask yourself, what is the shared goal they need to strive toward? Why should they care?
2. Identify objective, measurable, observable details indicating that their behaviors are insufficient.
3. Plan how to encourage their input toward course-correcting behaviors and support systems.
4. Clarify who is going to do what by when—and appropriate consequences for falling short.

Consider all the tips and tools in this chapter to help you develop and unify your team to make it easy to achieve your collective goals. Laying this groundwork makes it easier to refine the functional processes that we'll review in the next chapter.

SECTION FOUR

Prepare Your Outcomes

7

Margin for your Mission—Delivering Operational Excellence

"No margin, no mission"

– Irene Kraus, Daughters of Charity National Health System, who used it to explain that her hospitals couldn't rely on charitable donations alone.

How long would your medical facility be able to stay operational if you stopped making enough revenue to pay for salaries and facilities expenses? How many patients would suffer if your organization no longer was viable and was forced to shutter its doors?

In recent years, numerous healthcare businesses, both for profit and not-for-profit, have suspended their operations because they did not function with sufficient revenue to pay their operational bills. And the effects, especially in more remote communities, have been devastating.

While it is easy for a clinician whose passionate mission is to help those in need to feel frustrated by anything that smacks of the business side of the operation, the raw truth is: "No margin, no mission." Unless your team gets more involved with how to generate more effective and efficient ways to deliver your function, your influence will diminish and eventually stagnate. The time is now to take more control over your controllables and prove your strategic value.

Let's dig into the most vital considerations for your success in operational excellence.

Just Who Decides Whether It's Worth It?

Imagine if you asked the following question to your patients: "On a zero to 10 scale, how likely is it that you would recommend us to a friend or colleague?" What do you think they would rate the overall experience at your hospital? What do you think the primary reasons would be for their score?

What about asking your colleagues to recommend your organization as a place to work? What rating would they give? What do you think the primary reasons would be for their score?

According to a multi-decade research study conducted by business strategist Fred Reichheld and published by *Harvard Business Review*,[35] those who would rate you a nine or 10 are considered "Promoters," willing to not only return as a loyal customer, but also serve as an advocate to spread their personal testimony to those they influence. Those who rate you a seven or an eight are considered "Passives," who, while not quite loyal, are willing to return—unless their attention is distracted by another, more intriguing offer from a competitor. Finally, those who rate you a six or lower are considered "Detractors," who not only are dissatisfied with their overall experience but are more than willing to complain—actively trash-talking your organization on social media whenever the opportunity arises.

Ultimately, your collective success is determined by what the customers think about their experience—and how that influences their willingness to come back and/or tell those they know about your operation. As mentioned in previous chapters, the external "customers"—patients and their families—will shape your reputation by sharing about the experience you delivered. In the same way, your internal colleagues' experiences working at your organization is discussed with their friends and family as well as other colleagues—and word gets around. The stories that are told, about both your patient and staff experience, greatly influence whether

---

[35] Reichheld, 2011.

people—patients or staff—choose your organization.

The great news is that you and your team can not only profoundly affect those experiences, but also develop innovative ideas that save time, effort, and resources—leading to investment in growing a healthier operation that helps more people.

And isn't that why you got into healthcare in the first place?

Let's explore how to help even more people—without burning ourselves out!

"Don't say you don't have enough time. You have exactly the same number of hours per day that were given to Helen Keller, Pasteur, Michelangelo, Mother Teresa, Leonardo da Vinci, Thomas Jefferson, and Albert Einstein."

– H. Jackson Brown Jr.

How to Be More Efficient Without Losing Your Soul

The best people to allocate resources aren't just the "bean counters," who are isolated in offices all day crunching the numbers. The people with the best insights regarding resources are those actively dealing with those resources daily—you and your team!

These days, everyone is frantically trying to do more with less at a faster and faster pace. More than half of all nurses report severe burnout—an "epidemic on its own"[36] —and 16 to 39 percent report effects of "compassion fatigue."[37] Obviously, this will have an impact on the patient experience, as well as the staff experience. Our current approach is simply not working.

We need to think and take action differently. In addition to the overwhelm/burnout coping tips and tool introduced in Chapter 6, world-class organizations favor a time-management tool called the Eisenhower Matrix. Named after its originator, President Dwight Eisenhower, the matrix aligns the two aspects most vital to consider regarding time management: importance and urgency.

---

[36] Nigam et al., 2023.

[37] Walters, 2022.

As you can see from Figure 7-1, the matrix is divided into four quadrants, each reflecting a different combination.

Figure 7-1. The Eisenhower Matrix

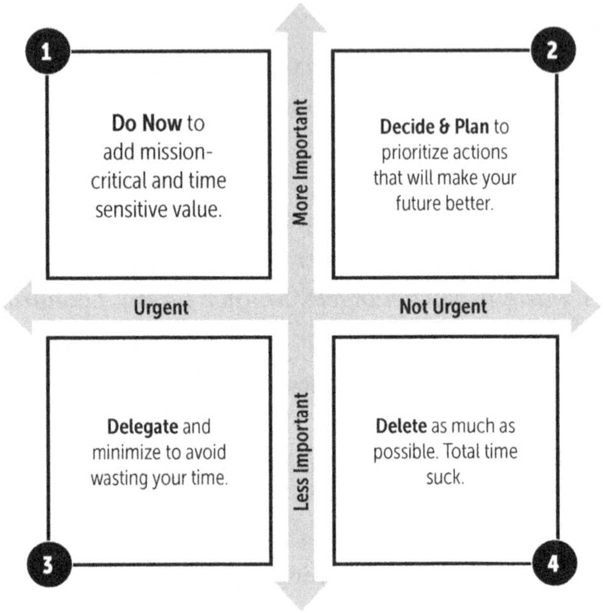

Here's a quick overview of the combinations:

1. **Important and Urgent:** This both aligns with your team and organizational mission and needs immediate attention. Drop everything and make sure this is a top priority.
2. **Important, but Not Urgent:** Make this a priority on your schedule to invest strategic effort to improve anything that can be improved. Think professional development, strategic planning, creating helpful templates that can save time and effort, and so on.
3. **Not Important, but Urgent:** Delegate or minimize what you can, as this is a non-mission-critical distraction and not a good use of your limited time.
4. **Not Important and Not Urgent:** Delete as much of these activities as possible; they are a total time suck.

The strategic goal is to identify the tasks you do and assign them to one of the four quadrants. Because only the activities above the horizontal line are deemed important, your aim is to delegate or delete anything below that line, then reinvest that time into the top-right quadrant of mission-aligned actions that help improve other efficiencies—and make your life better.

Early in my professional career, I was a paramedic with a fire-rescue unit. A typical day at that fire station team revolved around "Important, but Not Urgent," or quadrant two. Although I'd originally assumed that firefighters' primary job was to put out fires and save people, I was surprised to witness that they spent most hours training and maintaining equipment. They also did other (in my mind, originally) "non-firefighter" things, such as teach community groups about refreshing the batteries in smoke detectors and not using any potential fire hazards near Christmas trees. It didn't take me too long to realize that their efforts to strategically preempt problems saved time (and lives) as a result. Lesson learned? Being smart with your time to get fully prepared *before* it gets hectic pays massive dividends when the "stuff hits the fan".

So, how do you *implement* the Eisenhower Matrix tool? Individually, and then as a team, list out the various demands of your time and assign them to the appropriate quadrant. Next, brainstorm ways to minimize any activities in the "Not Important" quadrants, by either delegating them to those who are more legitimately aligned with it for their mission or deleting the activity altogether (Table 7-1).

Table 7-1. Recalibrating Your Time Resource

Do	Decide
▪ What "fire drills" happen most often? ▪ How can you prepare in advance for the most predictable aspects?	▪ What strategic time investments will best develop your key relationships or results? ▪ How can you maximize the time you invest here?
Delegate	**Delete**
▪ How can you best minimize the time required by these low-value activities?	▪ What "yes" opportunities justify you rejecting these time-wasting actions?

Some things to consider:

- Some tasks on your team's workload are likely determined by other people. If this is the case, you will need to have a logical rationale for requesting changes to the current workload assignment, and influence that decision maker to support the change—and make it worth their effort. Get crystal-clear about the operational demands and the political dynamics. (The influencing tool in Chapter 4 and the styles and needs tools in the next chapter will help you navigate that process.)
- Certain activities may seem non-mission-focused but are vital to relieving stress so you can be at your best when you need to be. Don't throw those particular tasks out. Place them in the "Important, but Not Urgent" quadrant. Ask: "Does this activity *really* make the best difference it can for my healthcare calling?"
- Also consider the time you spend complaining about things that aren't working well—both talking and merely thinking about them. It is significantly better to invest a bit of time fixing the problem, and then enjoy all that time back afterward. I like to think of it as (finally!) moving a coffee table that I kept stubbing my toes on. At some point, it becomes far better to confront the problem than to deal with the excessive pain and suffering of letting it continue.
- The more time and energy you save from the "Not Important" quadrants and reinvest into the "Important, but Not Urgent" quadrant will ultimately decrease the crises and fire drills you have to deal with. Eventually, with some initial extra effort and discipline, you will find your daily workload easier—freeing you to begin doing all the aspects of your healthcare role that you've always wanted to.

"If we excel in anything, it is in our capacity for translating idealism into action."

– Charles H. Mayo

Ain't Nobody Got Time for That

To be most effective with your time, it is critical that you master the art of saying no! William Ury, the author of the classic book *Getting to Yes*, also wrote a book dedicated to helping you become fluent in "the power of a positive no." In it, he states, "When we know how to use it correctly, this one word has the power to profoundly transform our lives for the better."[38] It is impossible to say yes to all the meaningful priorities in life unless we say no to the less meaningful distractions.

The first thing to recognize is that you have far more control of how you manage your time than you may believe. While there are always consequences for our decisions, you hold the power to accept or diplomatically decline requests for your time. Having healthy boundaries is vital in all aspects of our lives, and this is an important one. The best leverage for saying no, in my opinion, is to emphasize the more important and meaningful activities as a justification for not committing to misaligned requests for your valuable time.

> You have far more control of how you manage your time than you may believe.

Appropriately saying no is much easier when you are prepared. Using the Eisenhower Matrix to determine the best use of your time is a start, but you need to stop taking on new "not important" activities in addition to deferring those already on your plate. Some find it helpful to practice saying no in their personal life first, then transitioning that skill to their work life. Invest some time (quadrant two—Important, but Not Urgent!) in a self-audit of your activities, identifying those that don't work well for you—especially if they happen repeatedly. One no at a time will eventually open up a lot of time for those yeses you've been wanting to begin!

---

[38] Ury, 2007, 7.

SELF-EXAM

Review your calendar from the past month and identify anything that you regretted afterward. Clarify the true cost of taking that misaligned action (sacrificed needed time for your health or family, etc.). Review your calendar for the coming month. Are there any requests you can foresee that you should say no to? What diplomatic response would retain the relationship while clarifying your healthy boundaries? Even a simple "I'm flattered you asked, but I need to decline. I have other commitments that don't allow me to take on more right now. You might consider __________ as an alternative" can reflect your willingness to support without committing your time in the process.

Prioritizing Wins for Long-Term Success

When I directed leadership and change initiatives at Disney, I encountered several trends regarding challenges most organizations face—particularly when having to generate improvement momentum during challenging times.

Three interrelated tools lead to dramatic breakthroughs—driven by implementing small, consistent wins that generate momentum and inspire confidence in your team to keep facing down the challenges they are dealt every day.

Tool One: Categorize

The first tool is to categorize and clarify the many demands competing for your attention, and that of your staff. We found the solution in the Eisenhower Matrix.

Tool Two: Organize

The second tool is to brainstorm low- or no-cost solutions with your team, who are more aware of the details of your operation (and the patient experience) than anyone, so you can begin organizing them. There are many ways to generate ideas, but my personal favorite is the "Continue-Stop-Start" activity in Chapter 6.

Tool Three: Prioritize

The third tool is to prioritize. Most leaders make the mistake of focusing on the "sexy" ideas that come up, which are usually expensive and require budgetary approval, or complicated, requiring multiple functions and/or steps to achieve. Pursuing changes with this method will usually take a long time, all while the team wonders, "Whatever happened to that idea we had that leadership said they were going to implement?" That wondering eventually turns into frustration and feelings of betrayal—not exactly a formula for a healthy staff culture.

"To solve big problems, pursue small wins."

– Mark David Jones

Instead, triage by how easy or difficult they'll be to implement, with the intent to start your improvement efforts by focusing on the fastest "wins." This is far superior to other methods that most teams attempt. When your team sees a pattern of quick wins (idea one achieved on day one, idea two achieved on day three, idea three achieved on day seven, etc.), it naturally generates momentum and enthusiasm that this change effort is the real deal.

Bonus benefit #1: When people feel like their ideas are heard, valued, and implemented, this primes the pump for them to share more valuable improvement ideas.

Bonus benefit #2: Even the most cynical person on the team will notice that this approach is better after four or five quick-win improvements have been implemented and begin to get involved.

Bonus benefit #3: Constantly engaging your team to generate improvement solutions will not only save money and resources and grow your business (better-satisfied patients refer other patients!), but also shape your team culture to be more dynamic and growth-oriented for sustainable future success.

And the best part? You can use these three tools to improve your staff experience as well—which will transform your internal activities to position your team to best care for your patients.

When implementing these proven tools, you set the stage for making excellence easier and achieving your optimal potential—an exciting way to begin a new chapter for your team!

It Can Be, and Should Be, Better—Let's Start

"There's a way to do it better. Find it."

– Thomas Edison

To improve anything that involves humans, we need to understand all the components of their overall experience, from beginning to end. One popular approach is what some call a "journey map" or an "experience blueprint." This can be helpful to spotlight opportunities to improve at each step of the process, but it often falls short of guiding the improvement with the details that matter most to your patients. Remember, their overall opinion about the care you provide them is the culmination of *everything* they perceive at every touchpoint in their experience.

So, how can you make it easier to provide the meaningful healthcare experience you got into this career to deliver?

World-class organizations have discovered ways to go beyond the customer-journey-map concept to include the criteria that each unique customer (patient) has at each step of the experience. This ensures that you are targeting solutions that matter to those who are deciding whether it is worth it.

Details matter! And the details that your patient cares about matter most!

Details matter! And the details that your patient cares about matter most!

The best solutions can be determined only by appropriate criteria. Generally speaking, a high-level test should be a balance of:

- Does it improve the *patient* experience from their perspective?
- Does it improve the *staff* experience from their perspective?
- Does it improve the *operational and financial resources* of the organization?

This "three-legged stool" is a helpful way to start the conversation. To continue the process of refining your team's thinking, the next series of questions takes into consideration how well a proposed solution aligns with your unique organization. The following are examples of alignment questions used by the Mayo Clinic that you can adapt for your team's consideration:[39]

- "Is it consistent with the Mayo Clinic vision and core competencies?
- Does it reinforce the brand attributes, essence, and values patients and consumers associate with the Mayo Clinic?
- By user and industry standards, would it be judged among the best in its category?
- Does the service, product, or relationship deliver the benefits patients and consumers say they expect from Mayo Clinic?"

Like every other tool and example in this book, please approach this list with an attitude of *adapting* it to your unique circumstances. Clarify the criteria that work best for your situation. Once you have your questions developed, keep them front of mind as you explore, discuss, collaborate, refine, and land on your final decision for action. As you test and adjust during implementation, refer to them often to ensure you stay on the most effective path toward your extraordinary results.

The Foundation of How to Get There from Here

In 2024, Microsoft reclaimed their position as the most valuable publicly traded company. Overtaking Apple, which had earned that spot for years, was the consequence of CEO Satya Nadella's company-wide transformation, which was founded in shifting the company's culture. For years, Microsoft

[39] Berry and Seltman, 2008, 217.

was mired in a "know-it-all" culture—full of hyper-intelligent and skilled professionals. But that mindset had gradually become a barrier to growth. It's been said that "a strength overdone becomes a weakness." Microsoft realized that resting on their laurels had made them stagnate and vulnerable to their competitors' innovations. To turn this around, Nadella realized that the only sure way to continuous growth was to nurture a "learn-it-all mentality" instead. Microsoft provided tools (like those in this book) to help teams approach their challenges as opportunities to experiment with more innovative solutions, based on calculated risks focused on the user experience. Microsoft discovered during this process that empathy (like healthcare's core driver of compassion) was the key not only to better internal communication and team relationships, but also to a better understanding of their customers' deeper needs.[40]

There's nothing "soft" about the skills that generate superior outcomes. Leveraging both the relationship-building and results-building tools of the best organizations is simply doing what has been proven to work. Keeping this in focus as you begin constructing and implementing your improvement plan will ensure that you break through the barriers that most fail to overcome. It's the best way to make the difference you want to make in healthcare.

Your Plan Details for Getting There from Here

We're at a point where you need to start putting this book's tools together to orchestrate your efforts in a manageable way. Over the years, these tools have evolved to become what I call, simply, the Experience Sequence. When I use it to organize a plan for patients, it's called the Patient Experience Sequence (Figure 7-2, page 147), and when I use it for teams, it's referred to as the Team Experience Sequence. Here are the components for the patient experience:

- **The process steps:** Start with chronologically listing the steps of their experience with your team, from the first contact to the last. Each step in this sequence is an opportunity for them, and you, to make decisions about their experience.

[40] Hobson, 2024.

PRO TIP

Ever notice patients sometimes arrive with an "attitude"? If you engage them in the middle of a process, their demeanor is created prior to seeing you so prepare accordingly. (Also, consider touchpoints after you transfer them to the next team.)

- **Current patient touchpoints:** For each step in the patient process, get specific about when and how you and your team interact with the patient. These touchpoints include where people interact with them, as well as when they experience the environment (physical or virtual), and the policies or procedures. [And, if you are involved in the products they are exposed to, you could include products as well for bonus points.] What is their current experience? Examine how each of these delivery systems [which we'll explore in more detail in the next chapter] affects the patient to get a better, more three-dimensional grasp of exactly what is happening—and not happening—for them.
- **Patient expectations:** The ultimate criteria for success are in the minds and hearts of those you serve. Remember that they are feeling uncomfortable with the temperature, the strange sounds and smells; they don't understand the Latin or acronyms you're using, and they are scared by the unknown processes and/or outcome. You need to include their perspective and preferences, so adding your best understanding of them becomes part of this improvement tool. (Chapter 8 has additional information and tools to help complete this component.)
- **Your team values:** Including your values (in alignment with your organization, as discussed in Chapter 5) in this effort will keep your actions in sync with the overall nature of the experience you want to create. Patients notice, sometimes subconsciously, whether your team behaviors are aligned.
- **Low- or no-cost actions that *exceed* expectations:** At each step,

based on patient expectations, you can begin to identify simple "value-added" actions that can address the tsunami of emotions your patient experiences. That said, it is often the simplest and lowest-cost acts of caring—a friendly smile, a reassuring touch, a kind word shared at a meaningful time—that can significantly moderate their visit to your healthcare organization. When you are guided by your values and vision and consider the deeper needs of those you serve, it points your improvements in the most beneficial direction. Be guided by how you want them to *feel* while you are attending to their clinical needs.

- **Benefits of the new actions:** This provides an easily referenced reason for taking this particular action at this moment in the patient experience. How do these actions improve their experience? Their recovery? And how do they help you realize the impact you want to have as a healthcare professional?
- **Metrics:** The only way you really know if you are making progress in the way you intended is to measure your efforts. What easy ways can you more objectively track your behaviors or look for trends and patterns to reinforce your decisions? This is critical for testing and adjusting your efforts most efficiently.

PRO TIP

When deciding which metrics to track, keep in mind the existing measurements that senior leadership already tracks (so you know they value them) and align to them..

BONUS PRO TIP

Scan the annual report or the most recent strategic plan to guide your improvement choices, as they will become more easily justifiable (and more likely to be supported) moving forward.

- **Patient feedback:** One vital, albeit subjective way to receive input is to get real-time opinions from the patient. One benefit of asking—in a natural, conversational way—how they are doing, and about more specific aspects of their experience is that it shows you care, which itself can raise satisfaction levels. Some particularly helpful questions include "How are we doing with your care today?" and "I want to make you as comfortable as possible. Is there anything frustrating you today?"

Table 7-2. Patient Experience Sequence

Process Step (Decision Points)	1.	2.	3.	4.	5.	6.
Current Touchpoints ▪ People ▪ Place ▪ Process						
Patient Expectations ▪ People ▪ Place ▪ Process						
Our Values: 1. ________ 2. ________ 3. ________ 4. ________						
Low- or No-Cost Actions to Exceed Expectations						
Benefits of New Actions						
Metrics						
Patient Feedback						

Like any tool, the best insights come from the resulting team discussions. Of course, before you initiate that discussion, it is always helpful to draft out your thoughts in advance so you can lead the conversation most effectively. Here are some implementation tips:

- Set the context with your team (in your own words) that this activity is intended to use this tool to optimize the patient experience so it is easier for you all on a daily basis (less stressed patients are *far* more enjoyable to care for) and you can enjoy delivering the kind of meaningful care that led you each to start a career in healthcare.
- Clearly state that you expect their input and involvement. They have the best, most tangible experience with the patients you care for, so their insights and ideas are vitally important, which is why their involvement and input are so valuable.
- The first time you use this tool, you'll be drawing from previous patient experiences. Recall any trends, behavior patterns, comments, or incidences that can guide your team to the best starting place, then refer to the tool often to adjust with current patient input until it becomes an accurate reflection of the overall experience. The benefit of this tool is that it is completely adaptable to the ever-changing circumstances you may face in the future. The more you understand each facet of the patient experience from their perspective, the easier you can align your plans and actions to generate the very best outcomes.
- Leverage the previous tools introduced (plus those in the next chapter) to guide your ideas toward those that will be the best fit. One concept that can make this process easier is called "Freedom Within a Framework."

Freedom Within a Framework

The Freedom Within a Framework (Figure 7-1) concept represents that there are certain issues that are relatively firm: laws and regulations; safety and ethics; your company's non-negotiable mission, vision, values, and standards of excellence. These aspects are the framework. Anything that exceeds those parameters is out of bounds, or unacceptable. While this establishes a measure of limitation, it also provides helpful structure and *focus* as to what you should all be doing. The freedom aspect is anything within the framework. There are almost always more viable options than not. Yes, we all have guidelines, but the best leaders recognize that untapped opportunities are accessible through resources and appropriate options for conducting your day-to-day operation.

Figure 7-2. Freedom Within a Framework

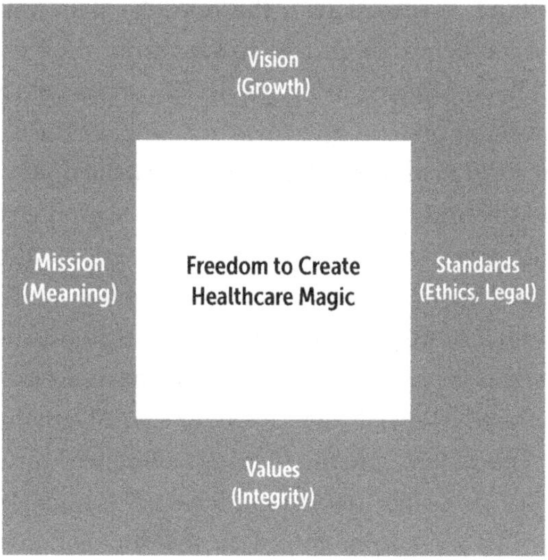

Anything within the framework is your playground for creating new ideas and exploring innovative solutions. What happens within these guidelines is valuable learning. What happens outside these guidelines is wasted time and resources. Think of your work and life as a garden. Anything that doesn't align or contribute to your dreams is a weed and needs to be pulled. If you wait too long to manage the weeds, it gets more difficult to maintain your garden. Once you do the initial groundwork to ensure less weeds, maintenance gets much easier. Do a sloppy job with the foundation, and you'll end up wasting precious time and effort on the weeds instead of nurturing, improving, and enjoying your garden.

Plush-Toy Wow, Part Three of Three

The housekeeper getting recognized for wowing her guests isn't the end of the story—for Disney. The benefits continued expanding as the housekeeping team for that floor started a friendly competition to see who could come up with the most innovative low-cost experience enhancing ideas. Various pleasant surprises, such as arranging other items in creative ways and leaving branded messages on sticky notes, began to earn a surge of complimentary guest letters.

Another unexpected benefit was the widespread action that this experience sparked. It started with the housekeepers from other floors of the hotel, who'd heard about this success from their managers. Each floor started collaborating to bring the Disney magic alive in their own ways. During the next general managers' meeting, all the other GMs were intrigued by the sudden improvement in guest-satisfaction scores. The story was shared and the other GMs, in turn, shared it with their housekeeping leaders at their respective hotels. The impact was suddenly magnified across two dozen hotels as the satisfaction levels rose dramatically for guests throughout the entire Disney property. A single gesture by a frontline housekeeper *who never even saw her customer* sparked a movement across the entire organization that elevated awareness, involvement, engagement, extraordinary experiences, and the "Disney Difference" service culture.

Responses like this often result from low-cost actions applied with an understanding of the guest, some guided, creative thoughtfulness, and sincere care. Your team of healthcare professionals already has these resources. When you create a culture that supports this approach and consistently implements it, not only should you expect the improvement process to get easier; you are likely to inspire breakthroughs for other teams as well!

SELF-EXAM

How can you focus on delivering more pleasant surprises, more enjoyable moments that exceed expectations, and more experiences that make patients completely satisfied and loyal?

Ways to Make the Process Easier and Better

Years ago, I was speaking at an event alongside the late and legendary General Electric leader Jack Welsh, who said, "Innovation is simple: Find a better way, every day." In his trademark cut-to-the-chase manner, he made it clear that improvement was everyone's responsibility and required daily attention. But to accomplish this, we all must work together using the same unifying approach.

Delivering effective clinical care involves complex reasoning and decision making. Until a couple of decades ago, human factors engineering (HFE) was often the primary means for analyzing the work of nursing. In 2004, a medical research team published an improved approach that combines HFE analysis with qualitative observation to develop the ADPIE model, which has become the methodology standard for analyzing the nursing process.[41] This model has helped medical-care professionals better navigate an often hectic environment to minimize disruptions to the nursing process that contribute to errors in decision making. ADPIE stands for the following:

- **A**ssess: Gather info/review history
- **D**iagnose: Identify a problem list
- **P**lan: Develop goals, desired outcomes, and an action plan
- **I**mplement: Perform actions
- **E**valuate: Were the desired outcomes/goals achieved?

This model provides a helpful path for progressing logically through any clinical improvement effort, but as much as I respect it, it also seems a bit close-looped—by which I mean it supports a comprehensive treatment process, but fails to contribute to the rest of the clinical team's edification, limiting any learning that occurs during the process. (Request to all my nurse colleagues: Please receive this in the "I'm solidly in your corner and your biggest fan" spirit that I'm suggesting it.)

I would humbly suggest adding two more steps to help close the gap: **S**hare and **R**epeat.

---

[41] Potter et al., 2004.

- **Share:** Whatever was learned in the process, make sure others on the team and anyone else who is related to the activity are aware of the result. You've invested time and effort (and budget) in gaining new knowledge and experience. Sharing the new insights multiplies the benefits.
- **Repeat:** Continuous improvement requires implementing this process, well, continuously! The more your team practices these steps, the more comfortable they become, and the more they develop the improvement skills required to succeed in this ever-challenging world of healthcare.

Since clinical care is a team activity, it is advantageous to share the outcome of the experience with the other care team members involved so they benefit from the process. It's the only way we can build on each other's improvement efforts and, ultimately, make our future better for everyone.

PRO TIP

One simple way to track trends regarding your improvements efforts is to record brief daily notes on the following three questions: 1. What worked well (and why) that we should repeat? 2. What didn't work well (and why) that we want to avoid repeating? 3. What was an unexpected result of our efforts today?

After just a week or two, you will notice trend details that can dramatically help next choices!

High-Tech and High-Touch

Every day, it seems, we see technological breakthroughs transforming the landscape of healthcare: artificial intelligence, the Internet of Things, "smart pharma," remote patient monitoring, digital communication tools, metrics for everything, and more. While technology will continue to integrate into the human experience, and therefore the patient experience, we need to stay aware of a key reality: The patient experience isn't just a portal. Technology is a tool, not the *only* solution. The solution always involves people, behaviors, and appropriate therapies. The healthcare provider and their actions, the patient and their actions, the treatment (therapy, medications, surgery, etc.) time and its ability to work: All of these contribute to the outcome; it is never just the technology. Yes, you must stay current on the ever-evolving technological tools, but your mastery of the *people* side of care is always the most vital link to successful outcomes. Make sure that you are using the tool and that the tool is not using you.

This doesn't mean we can ignore the impact of technology—we just need to see it as the tool that it is. Like any other aspect of the patient experience, it can add value or take it away. As much as technology can create efficiencies overall, which is a good thing, it must be coupled with the real-world experience. When the virtual and physical aspects are combined masterfully, it can create a very compelling patient experience, which is the reason your services exist. While we must embrace technology (or be replaced by it), we must guide the best use of it in vital patient and staff experiences.

Where Clinical Magic Is Happening: Yale New Haven Hospital

One recent example of rapid adaptability based on just-in-time data is Yale New Haven's COVID-19 nurse-staffing model. During the pandemic, it became clear that the 1,540-bed Connecticut teaching hospital would quickly run out of beds and nurses based on the existing staffing protocol. Taking into consideration the temporary closure of their operating rooms and some clinics, they shifted their efforts toward a more flexible approach based on aligning nurse competencies and functional need.

According to Ena Williams, chief nursing officer: "Our model now is no unit left unstaffed ... In the old days, we would send (the nurse) home if they were not an ICU nurse, but now we are saying: You don't have to go home, you can function in this support role and here is how you can do that."[42] This new approach involves key

[42] Castellucci, 2020.

stakeholders at every level of functional area and has become so successful that the nursing staff use it anytime they are temporary understaffed. These outcomes were produced by implementing the tools found in this book—particularly the learning/testing satisfaction measurement cycle. As of early 2021, Yale New Haven is using it to improve numerous other opportunities affecting the patient and staff experience across the entire operation.

"Ultimately, resourcefulness creates more successes than resources."

– Mark David Jones

You'll Never Have Enough Resources (Thankfully)

Most people have a misconception about how world-class organizations can succeed year after year. One common assumption is that these companies have all the resources they need to get the best results. As I look back on all the teams I led at Disney and the transformation efforts I led at other Fortune 500 companies, I can confidently say that is unfounded. Anytime I've asked someone at Google or Amazon or Apple (or Mayo Clinic or Cleveland Clinic) if they had enough budget or people or time to successfully achieve their project goals, they've *all* responded with a pained laugh and some explicit version of "Not even close." But that never stops them. They find solutions despite those limitations. And that's a blessing in disguise.

Now, don't get me wrong—at some point, insufficient resources will spell disaster for a project. But just because dynamic, accomplished corporations have earned huge profits doesn't mean they simply throw money at their problems. That never leads to long-term success. Instead, they get better, more innovative outcomes when teams are "forced" by circumstances to get creative. To push themselves. To create faster or more efficient processes, or the ability to complete a task with fewer people so they can be redeployed to other, more strategic tasks. Being "forced" to make do with less is often the recipe for getting skilled at being resourceful, which builds resilience, discipline, and innovation—all extremely valuable characteristics for any healthcare team in today's topsy-turvy world.

Amazon's founder, Jeff Bezos, has said, "'Accomplish more with less. Constraints breed resourcefulness, self-sufficiency and invention.'"[43] His 'Jeffisms' have become known throughout the company. No one likes to hear these truths, because they create a slightly uncomfortable situation. But as long as these goals are appropriate and properly supported (meaning that the entire team supports the purpose of the sacrifices and knows that their leadership will also be sacrificing in an equal, if not more impactful, way), then team members are more willing to do this for reasonable amounts of time: usually shorts bursts, with sufficient time afterward to revitalize. At Amazon, employees are guided by a set of rules: "Customer first, innovation always and long-term over short-term."[44] While these guidelines sound like superficial buzzwords, Bezos makes sure his teams consistently bring those values to life daily by serving as a role model. He still encourages customers to email him directly if they have a complaint. His passion regarding the mission and culture of Amazon is why their workforce is so willing to commit to those same demanding responsibilities—despite the challenge. Amazon's culture of honesty and consistency resonates with employees who are committed to the company motto: "*Gradatim Ferociter*," which is Latin for "Step by Step, Ferociously."[45]

SELF-EXAM

What insights for your healthcare team can you glean from this Amazon example?

---

[43] Meis, 2018.

[44] Ibid.

[45] Ibid.

Bloom Where You Are Planted

That said, the good news is that you are always in a position to make a difference wherever you are in your organization. You are likely someplace in the middle, looking for answers to make things better for you, your patients, and your team and organization. If this is the case, you should start by doing the following steps:

1. Focus on your own team. Although it is important to always be aware of the bigger organizational perspective, that is outside your current control, so it is more effective to focus most of your time and energy on your immediate team. There is plenty to do to improve you and your team, so start there. You are already intimately aware of almost every aspect of your team's function, dynamics, and challenges, so begin with that easily accessible opportunity.
2. Once you generate some momentum with improvements, start looking for ways to better influence people within your organization. Which decision makers affect your team most? How well do they know you? How much do they trust you? How credible are you to them? Do they believe you have their best interests at heart, as well as the overall company's? These are among the key issues you need to develop and improve to grow your influence and make a bigger difference in the future.

Focusing Your Team to Focus on Your Patients

Your team's raison d'être is to care for patients who need clinical help. Your team consists of professionals who, for various reasons, wanted to take the best care of people who desperately need their help. Your goal, as the team leader, is to reconnect them with that driving desire to make a difference and help them create the breakthrough that they've been wanting. But the solutions you co-create must ultimately connect to the reason you are all in healthcare: the patient experience.

8

"Heartwiring" Your Patient Experience

At the 2023 Forbes Healthcare Summit, Epic Systems' CEO Judy Faulkner had this to say about releasing a new artificial-intelligence tool to help clinicians make better decisions at the point of care by using de-identified data: "So far, our clinicians and patients have found that they like the AI's response better than the human's response because the AI is more empathetic."[46]

Does that finding disturb you?

Sounds like we need to put the human *care* back into *healthcare*!

Hospitals around the world have awakened to the reality that providing mediocre care is a fast track to obsolescence. Your competition is threatening. Technology is constantly reimagined. Regulations, insurance changes, reimbursement drama, facility needs, process coordination, pharma deliveries and storage, electronic health records, political pressures shifting back and forth ... and back again: The healthcare landscape feels like the emergency department during a full moon. The frenetic pace is numbing, and everything is in sensory overload.

And, in the midst of this mayhem, a nice little poster on the wall reminds us that the reason for all you do at the hospital is the patients.

---

[46] Perna, 2023.

How nice (he says, sarcastically).

From the beginning of your clinical education, it's been drummed into your head that the patient is all that matters—then, inexplicably, the "powers that be" immediately focus on all the medical "things" that make up healthcare interventions. Processes, medications, equipment, technology—they're all in service to the wide variety of patients you'll treat throughout your career. It's understandable that, with all the "shiny things" involved in healthcare, we often forget that the *patients* determine whether they follow your treatment plan, or come back for future treatment, or refer your practice to their family and friends.

While we have numerous impressive tools that contribute to excellence in care, world-class healthcare organizations have realized that patients perceive those details very differently from most clinical professionals (Table 8-1).

Table 8-1. Different Perspectives of Your Healthcare Experience

Healthcare-Experience Tools	Insider Clinical Perspective	Outsider Patient Perspective
Education & Training	Badges listing licenses, degrees, certifications, fellowships, and other recognitions reflect years of experience, positioning you as a knowledgeable and skilled professional in these specific areas.	Patients (and their families) *assume* you passed whatever standard required to work in a hospital. They hope you are one of the better practitioners, but generally don't know what all the acronyms mean.
Processes & Procedures	Over the years, your healthcare organization has established "how things work around here," and you and your team generally follow those clinical procedures.	Patients assume that everything is set up to achieve optimal results, but are confused by the unfamiliar sights and sounds. They don't understand why they're waiting when everything else is happening at such a hectic pace.
Equipment & Technology	We are impressed when equipment or technology is new (finally!), though quietly complain that it isn't more suitable for everyday applications.	Patients assume that the (intimidating) medical tools are there for a reason; they have no clue how the big imaging machine works, but accept it as part of the mysterious process.

Healthcare-Experience Tools	Insider Clinical Perspective	Outsider Patient Perspective
Treatment & Personal Interaction	Because we are focused on efficiency, coding, billing, and data entry (not enough time!), this aspect of the experience receives whatever time is left over from juggling all the other demands.	The only aspect of their care that patients are fully familiar with, and judge accordingly. If they don't feel you are listening to them, noticing their discomfort, or paying sufficient attention to them, they interpret this as "I'm not a priority. They don't care."

Not only is your patient's perspective different, but their expectations are different as well. Think back to five years ago. Are you a more informed customer now than then? Do you demand better service now? If you get bad service, do you simply go elsewhere? Do you tell more people about your bad experience now than you used to? Do you expect more value today than five years ago?

Not only is your patient's perspective different, but their expectations are different as well.

Shouldn't you assume that those you care for have the same higher expectations? What do you think they tell everyone about their experience?

We should all be very concerned about the experience we are delivering for them. The patient is the final arbiter of whether we succeed or not, so we must approach their care from their perspective.

Leadership expert Mark Sanborn, in his book *Up, Down, or Sideways*, writes, "Value is the currency of commerce...Individuals and organizations pay for what they value. And the organizations and individuals who get left behind in any economy are the ones that don't deliver what the marketplace [patients] values."[47] The challenge is that the "value" is a moving target! Because our role is to care for people, and people are constantly changing, the better we understand those we serve—whether our external patients or internal colleagues—the more likely we will succeed in delivering a valued experience.

---

[47] Sanborn, 2011, 82.

And thrive as a result.

I mentioned earlier that healthcare is not technically in the hospitality industry (ironic, given that *hospital* is the root part of the word *hospitality*), and should not strive to operate like a hotel. Yes, there are similarities (rooms, beds, people stay overnight, etc.), but the expectations and needs of a clinical patient are *far* deeper and more personal. Patients in hospitals are in acute to critical condition, meaning they are highly dependent and vulnerable. With that vulnerability often comes anxiety and raw emotion. The key to transforming your outcomes rests in engaging your patients more deeply and personally in a way appropriate to those intimate situations. Compassionate care requires understanding them in a more meaningful way.

Pursue What Matters Most

The healthcare industry is very competitive, but when you emphasize relationships characterized by care, respect, and clinical professionalism, you establish an advantage that others can't duplicate. Competitors can copy your remodeled admissions area or your slick marketing campaigns, but they cannot copy the personal bond you've established with a loyal patient. Loyal "customers" aren't looking to go elsewhere. They are so committed they often won't even notice your competition's attempts to woo them. Your goal should be that, when someone tries to convince one of your patients to try their provider, your patient cuts them off to explain that they are more than satisfied—and then encourage the other person to come to *their* provider the next time they need care. The best healthcare providers in the world have earned that kind of response. They will tell you it's a game changer. And that it is doable!

Generally speaking, the healthcare industry needs critical care itself. While you can't control the mayhem outside your organization, you can engage with the patient, who (eventually) determine your success. So, what makes highly satisfied patients?

Recently, the University of Utah Health conducted an in-depth study of patient feedback, identifying five key elements of the patient experience. They consist of the following (Table 8-2).[48]

---

[48] University of Utah Health, 2023

Table 8-2. Key Elements of the Patient Experience

Element	Theme	What It Looks Like to the Patient
Caring	Know Me	▪ Do they care about me as a person? ▪ Are they sensitive to my needs? ▪ Are they concerned about my questions and worries? ▪ Are they friendly and respectful?
Listening	Hear Me	▪ Do they include me in decisions about my care? ▪ Do they take the time to hear my concerns?
Explaining	Teach Me	▪ Did they explain my problem or condition? ▪ Do I understand my medications? ▪ Do I understand my follow-up instructions? ▪ Do they use language that I understand?
Teamwork	Coordinate for Me	▪ Was everyone friendly and courteous? ▪ Did my healthcare team seem well synchronized ? ▪ Did the team work together to care for me?
Efficiency	Make It Easy for Me	▪ How hard was it for me to get admitted? ▪ How long did I wait? Did they explain delays? ▪ Did they respond to my call light? ▪ How smooth was my discharge? ▪ Did they follow up with my other doctors?

When designing and developing your Patient Experience Sequence from Chapter 7, these patient-driven questions should be front and center for any plans you create to exceed their expectations.

> The saying "the customer (or in this case, the patient) is always right" is total BS.

One final comment I think is important to include here is that the saying "the customer (or in this case, the patient) is always right" is total BS. I'm not sure which MBA program came up with that ridiculous phrase, but anyone who deals with the real world knows it is nonsense. That said, the sentiment of the "customer's" opinion being important is completely valid. A more practical perspective is "the customer may not always be right, but if they are wrong, they *must* be wrong with dignity". The most skilled healthcare professionals find diplomatic ways to appropriately guide patients towards the truth so, throughout their experience, they feel respected and cared for.

What *Is* the Patient Experience, Exactly?

The patient experience is so personal—even invasive—that it has a strong emotional effect on the entire encounter. In fact, my healthcare clients have started calling their efforts to engage patients "heartwiring," to describe the attention given to this emotionally driven human experience. Unless the patient comes to the hospital regularly, it can safely be assumed that they will be having an experience that is extremely abnormal to them. They'll be compelled to talk about it. And because of this "emotional multiplier," it will certainly not be neutral. Knowing this, our responsibility is to pay attention to the details that matter most to them and ensure that your team delivers an experience that exceeds their expectations.

Here's one way to get and stay connected with the patient perspective, practiced by the Mayo Clinic. They regularly invite former patients to speak at lunch and learns or orientation classes to help staff understand the patient perspective more personally. This is a valuable approach whether their story is good or bad. For example, when I was working with their Phoenix hospital, they invited a former liver-transplant patient to one of the hospital's orientation programs, who had volunteered to share his experience with the new staff members. Not only did they gain insights about some specific procedural issues that could be improved, but they also received some helpful reminders about the emotional journey patients go through during this experience—and enjoyed the deeply-felt appreciation of the patient they had saved.

> The patient will determine whether it was worth it based on a blend of every component.

To exceed expectations in all aspects of the patient experience, world-class organizations have categorized the interaction into three primary aspects:

1. The people who are involved in delivering the experience
2. The place where the experience occurs (real world or virtual)
3. The processes that guide the experience

It's not enough that just one of these facets exceeds expectations. The patient will determine whether it was worth it based on a *blend* of every component. Again, the healthcare setting is uniquely intense for any patient or their family, so these details come under much more scrutiny than most any other experience.

The Front Line Equals the Bottom Line

For example, people who deliver the care experience should exhibit common courtesy: smiling, eye contact, tone of voice, and the like. Even the slightest of indicators can take on significance. J. Matthew Knight, M.D., president of the award-winning Knight Dermatology Institute, states, "Patients are really buying peace of mind when they come to the doctor. Patients should be able to see and feel your dedication to their safety."[49] My team says, "The front line equals your bottom line." Those on your team making direct contact with those you serve determine whether they come back—and what they tell others about their experience.

Keep in mind that everything is magnified by technology. Dr. Knight goes on to say, "Thanks to the internet, our patients no longer make appointments based chiefly on their primary care doctor's or family member's recommendation. Online reviews are overwhelmingly the main driver of patient appointments, along with locations and scheduling convenience. This means that your crew has to be laser-focused on the customer experience—from the moment a patient calls for an appointment to when they open your front door to when they're in the exam room to when they get a follow-up email thanking them for their visit. Owners who find that these exercises are beneath them are the same ones saying that they can't make it in medicine anymore."[50] In addition, "training and hiring practices are the keys to outstanding customer service. Training new hires on top-notch service is sometimes intuitive (i.e., follow the Golden Rule) but often requires one-on-one training and retraining sessions

---

[49] Knight, 2019

[50] Ibid.

aimed to hone strategies learned through trial and error and/or corporate best practices gleaned from other industries. You can train almost any employee how to inject Novocaine or work your [pain management] system, but you can't train someone to be sweet, compassionate, and considerate. A doctor's knowledge is important, but it's not as important as how customers feel about their overall experience."[51]

PRO TIP

When patients are overwhelmed (which is often), they respond best to their name, so refer to them personally and specifically throughout your discussions. This not only improves their comprehension of care directives, but also helps them focus on what you are trying to communicate. This simple addition to your interactions can increase their perception of engagement and personal care as well. What other simple changes can you or your team think of that can enhance the patient experience in big ways?

BONUS PRO TIP

Providing well-worded ways to communicate can be a beneficial tool; however, take care not to force scripts on your team. They usually come across as robotic and insincere. Instead, use guidelines and encourage each person to communicate those points in their own way.

SELF-EXAM

These details matter. How is your team making it obvious that they care about the safety of their patients? Is their compassion obvious? What about their professionalism? Their commitment to effectiveness? How are these traits reflected in your people, place, and processes?

[51] Knight, 2019

Everything Communicates

Your place also has a significant impact on your patients' experience. When was the last time you went step-by-step through the patient experience, examining what they see, hear, smell, taste, and touch? All of their senses will add to or take away from their experience's perceived value.

A number of years ago, I was working with a hospital and sharing insights about the importance of the physical environment to the patient experience. A VP of oncology insisted that the "niceties" of the waiting areas weren't important if the clinical treatment was executed properly. I asked her, from a patient-satisfaction perspective, how long the average wait time was for her department's patients, and how comfortable the waiting-room chairs were. She insisted they were comfortable ("We just bought them"), though admitted she had never sat in one. I challenged her to sit in one for the average wait time before declaring that the new seats were indeed comfortable—and thus adding to the patient experience.

A couple of weeks later, I got an email from her stating that she had fulfilled her promise and gleefully mentioning that the seats were even more comfortable than she'd expected. She then shared an even more important epiphany. She'd taken some paperwork into the waiting area with the intent of proving herself right about the seats, when a family walked in with a young boy who was starting his first round of chemotherapy. The VP described how she found herself thinking about things that I had shared and covertly started observing the family, who appeared nervous, as could be expected. She noticed they kept looking up, toward the ceiling. She followed their line of sight and saw that lining the perimeter of the waiting-room ceiling was a collection of plants—all withered and dying. She immediately realized that these parents, facing a life-and-death struggle with their young son, were surrounded by reminders of sickness and death. It didn't matter that the ability to inject the correct types of chemicals into the body was a totally different skill set from caring for mere plants (which were the responsibility of contractors, by the way). It still undermined the gut-wrenching experience of that family, and who knows how many others?

Another example of place having an impact on the patient experience is from the Mayo Clinic Labor and Delivery unit. A team member came up with the idea to play a soothing instrumental lullaby song to indicate to everyone on the floor that a baby had been born. Imagine how charming this must be to learn as a colleague—or even as a visitor to the hospital!

Ultimately, the biggest problem with issues in your physical environment is that they cause your patients to worry, which affects the experience—and even adds stress, which can undermine clinical outcomes. I've often heard comments from patients such as, "If their attention to details is so bad on [that insignificant thing I noticed], I wonder what their attention to detail is like when they are mixing the chemicals for my chemo?" I wonder what their attention to detail is like with the machine calibrations? The food in Dietary? The cleanliness of my room? When a patient's experience includes these kinds of things that chip away at their satisfaction, they will rarely become loyal—and will certainly not become advocates.

PRO TIP

Experience the (physical or virtual) environment from your patients' perspective. Sit in a wheelchair if appropriate, or kneel if they are children. Ask friends or family not familiar with your web portal to navigate it. What insights can you gain from seeing (and hearing and smelling) your facility from their perspective? What does it sound like at night? How can you adjust your patients' environment to communicate "compassionate professionalism"?

Make It Easy to Do Business with You

Finally, the processes your patients go through are part of their overall experience with your healthcare organization. Because of extensive regulatory demands, everyone has policies and procedures permeating every aspect of their operation. Many healthcare professionals make those processes the backbone of their clinical function, but neglect the care aspect as a result.

SELF-EXAM

Take an inventory of the various processes your team must adhere to. Identify what aspects of those policies were created to make the experience easier for the *organization*. What ways can those processes be reconsidered to maintain the safety and well-being of the patient but also make it easier for *them* instead? Is there another way to accomplish the goal of the process?

World-class healthcare organizations consider the impact of each guideline to ensure they don't make the experience more difficult for the (already overwhelmed) patients. This can be accomplished by shifting the ways that "unpleasant" aspects of the experience take place, so they are managed *away* from the patient, if at all possible.

Other times, patient ignorance becomes the problem—and it's a problem you can strongly influence! For example, one common patient complaint is that they don't get an immediate response when they ring the call system, even if the need isn't urgent. When pressed to provide more details, most patients share that they get anxious because they assume that the lack of immediate response means that if they *did* have an emergency, no one would come to their aid in a timely manner. Having a conversation with them in advance to manage their expectations is the key to resolving this concern—and preventing their incorrect assumptions from undermining their experience (and your reputation!).

PRO TIP

Note the most common patient complaints and develop how to proactively address those issues when orienting your patient. Start with assurances about your commitment to their care, then "inoculate" their expectations with a simple explanation about the complaint issue could occur and why, but that you will keep them a priority throughout their treatment.

BONUS PRO TIP

Fix the reason for the complaints and avoid the problem altogether.

Dr. Dirk F. de Korne, formerly the director of Singapore's KKH Children's Hospital, told me in 2018: [52]

> We are applying the [Disney] concept of "pre-show" to make the whole patient journey an attractive and interactive one. At KKH, we measure the different touchpoints with our patients and their families to nudge our colleagues to act on them. We have seen significant improvements because of leadership involvement, regularly monitoring of performance, and implementation of effective changes to improve our patients' experience. For our inpatient children wards, a structured bedside-handover program was developed to train our nurses to reduce caregivers' anxiety by getting the caregivers involved in the care plan and keeping them up-to-date on their medical care and patient condition. After a full rollout of the program, we have seen a significant improvement in the recommendation rate.

An Example of Bad Process That Got Shared on the Internet (A Lot)

We all are aware of the way the internet can draw attention, good and bad, to healthcare-industry experiences. Have you ever noticed how the passion of the comments rises with the degree of emotion created by the experience? Case in point: This description of a "worst customer experience" went viral a couple of years ago:[53]

> I'm going to say the front office at my therapist's clinic. I didn't get to go see her for almost a year because I was extraordinarily sick, moved, and injured myself while moving to the point that I had

[52] de Korne, 2018.

[53] Colin N., 2018.

> surgery. I called to make an appointment and they said that since it had been over a year, they had dropped me as a patient. Ok. So, do I fill out new patient paperwork again? Well, she's not accepting new patients right now. Ok, so can I see a different therapist because I'm seriously having some problems (they've got like 20 of them in the same clinic). Well, since you're established with her and you have a rapport built up with her, we don't want to switch you to a new therapist. You could try calling back next month, but just so you know she's booking four to six months out. At this point I get pissy and say, "Ok so I'm calling you guys because I'm having major issues. What if I was having suicidal thoughts? Are you going to tell a person with suicidal thoughts that they can't see a different therapist since theirs is booked till May?" And that's when she hung up on me. I called back and said, "Hey I think we got disconnected" and she hung up on me again. So yeah, a mental health clinic that hangs up on people that have a history of suicidal tendencies and are asking for help gets my vote.

Ouch! What damage did this have on the clinic? How many people do you think the patient told? How many people were told about the incident by people who read the viral social-media post?

This example illustrates a combination of process and people issues that is not patient-centric. Unless we systematically review and develop all aspects of our care with these perspectives, we will fall short of our healthcare calling.

The Delivery Systems in Action

The respected Cleveland Clinic established an Office of Patient Experience that "has been identifying best practices throughout the enterprise to streamline patient experience initiatives," along with a Best Practices Department.[54] Here are some examples of what they have done to enhance the patient experience:

- To improve patients' rest, and therefore healing, staff coordinated

[54] Cleveland Clinic, n.d.

a "Quiet at Night" team that created a "Help Us Support Healing" (H.U.S.H.) protocol, which reduces nighttime noise from 9 p.m. to 7 a.m.

- To help nurses anticipate patient needs and demonstrate staff availability to attend to those needs, the clinic instituted "Purposeful Hourly Rounding." This allowed nurses to manage their own time based on patient circumstances and be more effective in building positive, trusting relationships.
- Every month, leaders work in teams of three and are assigned to inpatient or outpatient locations to perform "Leadership Rounding." This hands-on activity helps them not only to gather feedback and information directly at the point of treatment, but also to translate new insights into action plans for improvement. In addition, the leaders report learning more about staff issues and developing improved engagement with them as well.
- The Office of Patient Experience, working with the Nursing Institute, launched "Effective Nurse Leader Rounding" to help manage patient expectations and promote quality care. They discovered that by role-modeling expected behaviors and recognizing exceptional caregivers, they saw a significant improvement in satisfaction scores from patients and staff.
- To prioritize responding to patient call lights, they created a "No Pass Zone" program that empowers all caregivers, not just assigned nurses, to acknowledge or even resolve the patient's needs.

We must also take care to do no harm to a person emotionally.

Most healthcare professionals are familiar with the industry philosophy of "Do no harm." Most of us emphasize physical harm. Our responsibility, as Dr. Charles Mayo once said, is to "the whole person," which means that we must also take care to do no harm to a person *emotionally*.

Regardless of what role you play in your healthcare setting, it is important to remember that the patients (and, often, their families) are vulnerable. Always. I'm sure you've noticed how people do squirrelly, illogical things when they feel susceptible and overwhelmed. The treatment that soothes this discomfort during those stressful times (and being in a hospital is always strange and stressful to patients) is compassion.

Of course, all the clinical procedures and behaviors you must perform to ensure safety and quality are still necessary for *how* you deliver care, but compassion is *why* you deliver care. Patients and their families typically don't understand all the details of clinical safety and quality, but they grasp whether you seem to care enough to be compassionate during their life-changing situation.

And they *will* remember. (Will they ever!)

SELF-EXAM

What insights can you take from these examples and adapt to improve your team operation?

Shifting From Knowing About Your Patient to Truly Understanding Them

The key thing to obsess over when creating a patient-centric experience is that their satisfaction is based on their *perception*—and their perception is almost always affected by their emotional state. Most patients are overwhelmed by the unfamiliar experience: They are confused by the Latin words and acronyms that they don't understand; they are uncomfortable; they have lots of unanswered questions and, in some ways, are not even sure what to ask; they are cold; they are concerned about their finances; their lives are being disrupted; their future less certain than it was when they were admitted; they are scared; they are disoriented by the cacophony of strange sounds; they don't understand why people aren't treating their situation with more urgency ... the list goes on.

I'm exhausted just writing about it.

World-class organizations have strategically used these steps to help them discover insights that make this process less guesswork and more purposeful. Two of the most helpful include one that reveals the deeper, prioritized needs that drive patients' decisions about their experience, and another that helps address each person's primary personality trait and how to "flex" our own to better engage them.

"Understanding human needs is half the job of meeting them."

— Adlai Stevenson

Years ago, my team was hired to consult with two client organizations in two very different industries; both wanted to launch large-scale culture-alignment initiatives. Both corporations hired big firms to conduct and analyze extensive surveys, interviews, and ethnographic studies, so they could better design a comprehensive approach to serving their customers most effectively. Both organizations did business worldwide, and thus worked with people of all cultures, socioeconomic statuses, and political leanings. Both entities spent millions of dollars independent of each other to arrive at their ultimate findings. Because I was in the unique position of guiding both efforts, I was able to see the findings of both reports. When I compared the two, I discovered that they both concluded that humans have the same five essential needs.

That certainly got my attention. And, if you deal with humans at all, it should have gotten yours.

"You will be your best self when you take time to understand what you really need, feel, and want."

— Deborah Day

The Five Essential Needs

These essential needs were first revealed to the public in the book *Lead With Your Customer: Transforming Culture and Brand Into World-Class Excellence,* written by myself and J. Jeff Kober.[55] These essential needs are

[55] Jones and Kober, 2019.

the foundational drives that motivate your patient or customer to decide whether what you offer is valuable to them.

They are the need to:

- Feel heard and understood
- Feel stable and in control
- Feel significant and special
- Feel they belong and contribute
- Feel successful and reach their potential

Note that these needs involve them "feeling" the fulfillment for them to consider them met.

> **SELF-EXAM**
>
> While we are exploring ways to better engage your patients, keep in mind that this tool also can help you better interact with your colleagues.

The first thing to notice is that these needs supersede concern for the specific products or services most organizations emphasize. While details such as what procedure we are doing with which instruments are important, the patients assume all of that is appropriate (again, it is all a mysterious "black box" to patients). What your patients *can* determine is why and how you engage them. They want to understand and feel confident that they are being treated by a team that cares about what matters most to them.

> What your patients <u>can</u> determine is why and how you engage them.

Regardless of what kind of human you are engaging, here are some more detailed insights regarding each of these essential needs to help you consistently exceed their expectations:

The Need to Be Heard and Understood

The first of the essential human needs is a concept that serves as a gatekeeper for all the others. Providing extraordinary, compassionate care to your patients begins with first understanding them. If we don't truly understand each other, we'll likely fall short of addressing the remaining needs.

It's common for most people in hectic environments (sound familiar?) to stop actively listening to someone once they assume they understand the key points. Even if you're correct in understanding the content of the conversation, if you don't address their deeper needs, you'll fall short of enabling the other person to *feel* heard and understood. This involves compassion—a vital component of engaging patients—so pay attention to the person's emotions. You don't have to share the emotion with the person (see Chapter 6, regarding behaviors that lead to burnout). Simply identify the emotion that they are experiencing in order to make an informed choice about how to best interact with them during their care.

This requires more than simply nodding in agreement or parroting back what they have just said. Try asking open-ended questions to get more details from them, then align your response to what you think they are feeling and what is really being said—even between the lines. Confirming your understanding during the discussion (without using their exact words, which can be annoying) can help them realize that you care enough to make the effort. Again, the key is not just that you do these behaviors; it's that the patients feel heard and feel understood. Have you ever had someone say, "Finally, someone gets where I'm coming from!"? This is a good sign that you've helped them feel heard and understood.

Breakthroughs happen when people sense that you really hear and understand them. Emotional walls come down and healthy relationships flourish. By successfully addressing their need to *feel* heard and understood, you set the stage for trust, engagement, and effective outcomes—the holy grail of every healthcare operation.

Something to consider: The patients who consult "Dr. Google" and lean on that information more than ours do so because they don't believe we are really listening to them or understand them, or they simply don't trust us, because we haven't sufficiently developed a good rapport with them. One healthcare client decided to stop fighting them and literally join them. They sometimes sit with the patient in front of a computer and Google the search together to get on the same page/better understand what the real concerns/facts are—and help the patient better understand what all the complicated information on the webpage means. Bottom line: With all the technology changes that are happening now in healthcare and given the concern of patients and their families about their health, we can expect that they will grasp at any technological tools they can access—and we need to include that dynamic in our strategies for leveling up.

PRO TIP

You've likely had active-listening training, which can be helpful, but please don't use the canned phrase "What I hear you saying is ...". If the person you are talking to has been in that training, it will come across as them "being techniqued" (one of my pet peeves!) and possibly interpreted as manipulative and insincere—not good for generating trust. Try more natural discussion responses for best results.

The Need to Feel Stable and in Control

Have you noticed how people react when they are in uncomfortable surroundings? It is easy to understand how much people desire feeling stable and in control of their circumstances. Providing stability as part of a clinical-care scenario can be accomplished in many ways. Despite the reality that life is imperfect and we are never 100 percent in control, we need to grasp that it is human nature to want to feel more stable in this uncertain world.

In the healthcare sector, it's hard to find many organizations that *aren't* dedicated to helping patients feel secure in times of need. And yet, that is the common problem reflected in public sentiment regarding a healthcare experience: a lack of peace of mind and assurance. Whether your patient has suffered through a pandemic or an accident or any other unexpected health incident, how is the outcome of care undermined if they are besieged with anxiety and fear? Is it possible that you can provide correct clinical treatment and still not meet your patients' needs?

PRO TIP

One quick solution to help someone feel more stable and in control is to offer choices. Even if they ask for something unreasonable—you can counter with, "We can't do (request A), because of (reason), but we can offer (option B or option C); which would you prefer?" Just offering a choice helps them feel more in control, calmer—and much easier to care for. Try it out!

The Need to Feel Significant and Special

Another fundamental human need is to feel as though we matter to others. The primary way that world-class organizations consistently accomplish this is to take time to understand their customers (or colleagues) and make an obvious effort to care for them in a personal way. For example:

- Taking additional time to hear customers' concerns, which is connected to the first need—feeling heard and understood
- Appropriately making exceptions to policies to care for customers' higher-priority individual needs
- Recognizing customers in a personalized way that's meaningful to them

When working to make people feel significant and special, keep in mind the way *they* want to be treated. Spending time with someone is the primary way to show you think they are significant. Of course, in healthcare, time is a resource in very short supply. That said, I like to use an "investment mentality" even in establishing relationships. Consider how you can take actions that create multiple "returns on investment," such as:

- Follow up quickly if they have a special request. If it takes longer than expected, explain in a way that emphasizes they're significant, like, "I'm sorry it took so long. I had to call in some favors [indicates you made an extra effort], but I hope you enjoy it."
- Think quality over quantity. Yes, you need to gather clinical data during rounds, but weaving in relationship-building conversation about why they want to get better improves hope (and, often, outcomes) and also engages them in a more meaningful interaction with you.
- Notice what is important to them. Do they talk about family? Weave their family into your talks. Ask (appropriate) questions. Show an interest in them as a human with a name rather than as "the [clinical procedure] in room two."
- Writing a handwritten note will have a lasting effect, beyond the initial reading of it. Many patients will read these notes multiple times throughout their recovery—even after they get home. In addition, family members will read them and may even post them on social media (so stay HIPAA-compliant!)

Make the effort to go beyond merely knowing *about* them. Their EHR chart shows only data regarding their medical condition. Get to know about them as a person, and you will create breakthroughs in helping them feel significant—and create superior engagement for even better outcomes. [There is a great tool for this later in this chapter.]

PRO TIP

Use the person's name if possible, as appropriate. This make the interaction not only more personal, but also more specific (you are informally confirming that you are discussing their unique situation). This often opens the door to them opening up more about their symptoms and can lead to a more accurate diagnosis or treatment.

The Need to Belong and Contribute

The next essential need your patients have is to belong and contribute in a meaningful way. We humans are social creatures, and throughout recorded history, people have gravitated toward living in communities. Friendships, families, even national pride are reflections of our common need to belong. It's easy to observe everyday behaviors that reflect this fundamental need:

- Cheering for your hometown sports team
- Buying products that "cool" people buy (Think brands like Apple, Starbucks, Cherokee Medical Uniforms, Bala Footwear)
- Buying American-made products only
- Joining social organizations such as the Rotary Club, or online social networks like Facebook's Nurses Rock Group or LinkedIn's RN Network-Nursing Community group

Are you an Amazon Prime member? (My peeps!) Have you ever provided feedback on any of their products or on their shipping status? When my team worked with them years ago, we learned that they purposefully created different ways customers could contribute to the "Amazon Experience." They had discovered through numerous metrics that people who volunteered to be involved in any activity (such as providing feedback and even filing a complaint) developed purchasing patterns that increased loyalty more than customers who never chose to interact with their brand beyond the purchase.

St. Jude Children's Research Hospital began a fantastic practice the year I started consulting for them. They offered an opportunity to patients' families, and later to financial donors, to buy a brick with their family name on it, which was then placed as part of a sidewalk called "The Pathway to Hope" in front of their hospital. This sidewalk has become so popular, it now surrounds almost the entire property (they had to conclude the program at the end of 2022). But their "fans" wanted more, so St. Jude now offers multiple walls across their campus in which to place a brick. Their "Heritage Wall" includes names in the lobby of their headquarters. In addition, they offer a "Wave of Thanks" wall in their main patient-care area that features plaques with encouraging messages, which patients, families, doctors, and visitors can see. People say that their experience there was so special that they wanted to *be a part of St. Jude.*

When people have a positive experience with your healthcare organization and are given the chance to actively contribute, they become more loyal as a result. Having "skin in the game" solidifies their connection with your organization. The more we understand the need to belong and contribute, the better we can address patient preferences in the experience we offer.

PRO TIP

When people feel that the experience they had with you was special, they want to stay connected. What creative ways can you offer those you serve to take a more active role in contributing to your success? How can you help them feel like they're a meaningful part of the profound difference you make in the lives of people every day? Give them the chance to be a partner in heroism and watch your fandom grow!

The Need to Feel Successful and Reach Your Potential

It is human nature to want to succeed. That said, success means different things to different people. There are numerous traits that support someone taking action to reach their potential, such as:

- The satisfaction of generating the courage to try a new skill for the first time
- The emotional discomfort of being dissatisfied with the current situation
- Enjoying the adrenaline rush that comes with surmounting difficult challenges

Of course, there are obstacles to reaching your potential as well, such as:

- Having previously experienced defeat

- Lack of encouragement or support
- The perceived risk of blame, embarrassment, or other negative consequences
- Oppressive team dynamics

Every day, you have the opportunity to help people reach their potential. Sometimes it will involve helping them start their effort or supporting a particular step in the process. Other times, it will involve helping them remove barriers or overcome adversity. Regardless, just being there to support them will not only help make things better, but also strengthen the trust and credibility you have with them. And that always pays off eventually, one way or another. It's a worthy investment!

Another thing to consider is what success means to them. It will be different for every person—and their idea of success will evolve over time. The best organizations in the world depend on leaders like you to engage others to discover their goals and help them achieve them—whether they are patients or colleagues.

PRO TIP

Dig deeper when doing intake on (non-urgent/non-life-threatening) patient cases. These patients will likely have to follow some directions regarding their recovery, which many do not follow effectively. To help motivate them to take a more active role in their own health, learn *why* they want to get healthier. Connecting their plan of care with a personal definition of success ("I want to pick up my grandchild") can make a profound difference in their recovery and ultimate outcome.

The Essential Customer Needs and Your Healthcare Team

To realize your healthcare purpose of helping others live their best, healthiest life, you need to understand and provide those things your patients (or your colleagues) need most. Creating a meaningful care experience is about more than providing products and services. It's about addressing the real needs of those you serve—both outside and inside your healthcare organization. Work with your team to identify what your typical patients expect for each of their five needs. What clues lead you to believe those opinions? What ways can you confirm or clarify your current opinions? What are some low- or no-cost actions to exceed those expectations? How can you make it easier to consistently exceed those expectations—even in the middle of a typical hectic shift?

PRO TIP

Consider those same questions, but for your team or those you interact with within your healthcare organization. How can you exceed the expectations of those internal customers?

Table 8-3 is a tool to identify ways you can exceed the expectations of those you serve—whether external patients or internal colleagues—regarding the five essential needs.

Table 8-3. Essential Customer Needs

The Essential Need to:	Their Expectations (And How Do You *Know?*)	Low- and No-Cost Ways to Exceed Expectations
Feel Heard & Understood		
Feel Stable & in Control		
Feel Significant & Special		
Feel They Belong & Contribute		
Feel Successful & Reach Potential		

Brainstorm ways that these five essential needs show up at work and how to create effective ways to meet them as part of your daily operation.

"My personality traits don't determine my destiny. They inform it."

— **Anne Bogel**

Personality Traits Matter

Another key tool that helps you go beyond knowing about those you serve to actually *understanding* them is differentiating the distinct personality traits that are reflected across all cultures around the world and leveraging them to enhance your interactions with each person.

From the inception of the documented study of healthcare, the venerable Hippocrates (from whom we get the original Hippocratic Oath, which established the ethical responsibilities of clinical-care providers) observed that his patients reflected four different "personas." Each persona took a particular worldview, which heavily influenced their preferred responses and behaviors. The Greek physician noticed that each one required a different approach to best engage in an effective treatment. While his descriptions of them are understandably dated (his definitions are, after all, more than 2,000 years old—and in Greek), their validity and general meaning have been reliably observed in studies of human nature ever since.

You have likely taken some kind of personality indicator at some point in your professional career: Myers-Briggs Type Indicator, DiSC, True Colors, Keirsey Temperaments, Social Styles. While they all categorize human traits and preferences, most end up with four primary categories (even the Myers-Briggs' 16 types can be sorted into four sections). Table 8-4 has some comparisons to illustrate this phenomenon.

Table 8-4. Personality Traits

Hippocrates Personas	Myers–Briggs Type Indicator	DiSC Assessment	Keirsey Temperaments	General Types
Choleric	SJ	Dominance	Guardian	Mobilizer
Sanguine	SP	Influence	Artesian	Energizer
Phlegmatic	NF	Steadiness	Idealist	Sympathizer
Melancholic	NT	Conscientious	Rational	Analyzer

There are a multitude of books on how these different types of personalities prefer to operate and interact, and I encourage you to delve more deeply into them if you are interested. That said, here are some foundational insights that can transform your future interactions with both patients and colleagues:

- There is no one trait better or worse than any other trait. They are merely different.
- It is human nature, especially in times of stress (and remember, people are under an unknown amount and type of stress in their lives) to revert to whatever trait they feel most naturally comfortable with as a coping mechanism.
- You have a trait. Unless you are actively thinking about it, your habits will reveal your preference to everyone you interact with.
- It's not all about you. If you survey a standard heterogeneous group (not all engineers or cheerleaders), you usually find approximately 25 percent in each category—which means that about 75 percent of the time, the person you are serving or working with is *not like you*. They prefer to interact, communicate, learn, organize, make decisions, and so on in ways that align with their trait. To be most effective, you must be willing and able to adjust your own trait to engage effectively with their trait.
- You can learn to improve the way you engage others. Get familiar with those differences and consider how you might better frame your interactions based on their preferred trait. Table 8-5 includes some quick examples for each generic trait

regarding different functions; Tables 8-6 and 8-7 describe ways to effectively communicate with each trait.

Table 8-5. Typical "Default" Personality-Trait Preferences

Trait	Characteristics	When in Conflict
Mobilizer	Task-orientated. Typically prefers clearly defined goals. Perceived as committed, determined risk takers. Efficiently uses time, energy, and other resources. Seeks control and results.	Can be seen as impatient, aggressive, rude, or abrupt. Seems to "steamroll" others on occasion.
Energizer	People-orientated. Most comfortable when the center of attention. Typically positive, emotional, talkative, enthusiastic; can be dramatic. Seeks recognition.	High-energy. Can be viewed as unpredictable and emotional. Often the first to complain.
Sympathizer	Loyal, supportive, and patient. Uncomfortable with risk. Typically nonconfrontational. Dislikes pressure. Enjoys the company of others. Seeks security and harmony.	Likely to be considered "passive." Perceived as lacking conviction. Uses avoidance to reduce conflict.
Analyzer	Serious; mulls matters over. Can seem indecisive. Persistent, asks lots of questions. Known for heightened attention to detail. Seeks to be correct.	Can sometimes resort to sarcastic or biting negative comments; can seem "shut down" or be uncommunicative.

Table 8-6. How to Interact with Each Personality Trait to Improve Communication

Trait	Communication	Information	Decision Making	Organization
Mobilizer	Varies depending on situation	Cut to chase; facts/details	Practical and solution-oriented	Sticks to clear plans and deadlines
Energizer	In person, groups	Big-picture ideas and possibilities	Group values and impact on others	Spontaneous improvisation
Sympathizer	In-person; one-on-one	Big-picture concepts	Personal values and impact on others	Prefers flexibility and options
Analyzer	Usually prefers virtual	Concrete facts/ details	Logical process, fairness	Prefers rules, structure

Table 8-7. Understanding Personality Traits to Achieve Healthy Team Dynamics and Superior Results

	Mobilizer	Energizer	Sympathizer	Analyzer
Measures Personal Values By	Results	Recognition	Security	Accuracy (being right)
For Growth, Needs To	Listen	Check	Initiate	Decide
Wants Climate That	Allows them to build their own structure	Inspires them to reach goals	Provides details	Suggests
Takes Time to Be	Efficient	Stimulating	Agreeable	Accurate
Support Their	Conclusions and actions	Dreams and intuition	Relationships and feelings	Principles and thinking
Present Benefits That Tell	What	Who	Why	How
For Decisions, Give Them	Options and probabilities	Testimonials and incentives	Guarantees and assurances	Evidence and service
Their Specialty Is	Controlling	Socializing	Supporting	Technical

For a free assessment of this personality indicator, please go to ***ResultsStat.com/BookResources****.*

Once you gather insights about the different preferences of yourself and your colleagues, you'll be better at detecting clues from your patients about their preferred traits as well. This will help you customize any care plans you have for better results. Combine that benefit with a deeper understanding of their five essential needs, and you'll have a dramatically improved opportunity to engage them in a more meaningful and productive way.

PRO TIP

If you happen to be in a geographical area that has relatively predictable types of patients, it can be helpful to develop some patient "persona" tools that can serve as an initial shortcut to anticipating how to best initiate the interaction. (Note: As mentioned previously, this is not intended to be a way of stereotyping anyone. These traits are merely a method to better understand the differences of the people you serve and work with.) Start with the four personality traits detailed in this chapter and create examples of how each trait may prefer to be cared for. This can be a helpful tool to assess the actual preferences of the unique individual in front of you.

Note: *These "micro-tools" will dovetail into creating a larger, more comprehensive Patient Experience Sequence tool from Chapter 7.*

Creating Pleasant Surprises

All these proven tools have been developed solely to make it easier to consistently provide an extraordinary patient experience and deliver an unwavering commitment to excellence. Use them with the goal to create pleasant surprises. Something unexpected becomes a remarkable part of the patient experience (and one that they want to remark on to their family and friends). Here is an example of one client who tested a creative idea filtered through the tools from this book.

Van Dyk Health Care, in New Jersey, is an award-winning nursing home communities (Voted a Best Nursing Home repeatedly by *U.S. News & World Report*) that has a long history of adapting these world-class practices to improve their outcomes. CEO Bob Van Dyk shared one example of how using clear values helped identify a significant improvement to the process the organization follows when a resident patient passes away, and how they prepare all their belongings to give to the family.

A number of years ago, after the death of one particular resident who had been there quite some time, they provided the usual service of gathering all the belongings and placing them in a brown bag for a family member to pick up. The family member, who was often at the facility and had gotten to know the nurses and other caregivers, took the bag and, after taking a few moments to compose herself, gave the director some feedback.

She mentioned that they had become like family over the years and that she'd had many wonderful memories with the staff. It seemed sad that the people she had considered so dear to her treated her mother's belongings like they were trash in a bag. The staff were horrified at the thought and quickly brainstormed a relatively low-cost solution.

The team bought some sturdy cardboard boxes with a pleasant design on the outside and would then line the box with the resident's personal quilt and carefully arrange all their possessions in it. The staff members who'd interacted directly with the patient would then sign a handwritten card expressing their condolences and personal well-wishes to the family. This small change has resulted in a profound improvement on the "last impression" of the family members' experience and has led to, according to the nursing-home leaders, a renewed sense of pride among the staff, loyal family members who become advocates for their nursing home, and an enhanced reputation throughout the community.

SELF-EXAM

Which step in the typical process of being treated by your team could be enhanced by a creative "pleasant surprise" that is meaningful and demonstrates personal caring on behalf of your team? From your patient's experience? From your colleagues' experience? How can you prepare in advance to make the gesture easier—even when things are busy?

SECTION FIVE

Secure Your Future

9

Implementing Your Transformation

"The only way you'll successfully innovate is if you go out there and try. A lot of companies shy away from what looks tough. But you have to be fearless to attack these problems. You can't be afraid of failing."

— Dr. Gerald Hautman, Chief Medical Officer, UnitedHealthcare

If you've made it this far, I'm guessing you're serious about next steps—so here are some final thoughts, some case-study examples, and a checklist for your success (along with bonus final thoughts, at no extra charge).

Final Thoughts, Part One: Fulfill Your Healthcare Calling

"We cannot become what we want by remaining what we are."

— Max DePree

As healthcare professionals, we've all read books, attended seminars, listened to in-service sessions, and been given coaching during our careers. Why is it that, despite all this learning, most people still struggle with mediocre results? What is the differentiator that sets the highest-performing people apart? The answer is always in what they do *after* getting the learning. The most successful people get huge results because they take action and apply what they have learned.

In this book, I've shared behind-the-scenes success secrets from world-class organizations, outlining the most critical actions to take your team from ordinary to extraordinary. Your next step will determine whether you will reap the benefits of these insights. Taking action now, not later, will set you on a path to optimize your potential.

The very *un*-sexy "secret sauce" of every world-class organization is a combination of consistency and sustainability. Disciplined focus and unyielding effort are what lead every industry. The ingredient that ensures that the successes are long-term is sustainability—aligning with the World-Class Success Chain model (Chapter 3). Make these mundane concepts a priority throughout your journey, and you will realize your goals.

Disciplined focus and unyielding effort are what lead every industry.

Earning a reputation of world-class excellence is not easy, but it sure is satisfying to enjoy the results. Your future self and team urgently need you to start this effort. Making that little extra effort today leads to a better tomorrow. Repeating this daily creates a proven path of continual improvement, to exceed the ever-rising expectations of your patients and their families and beat your competition.

By following the step-by-step process included in this chapter and using the various tools supplied, you will begin building the team breakthrough you've been wanting. Even better, many teams have been the catalyst that sparks an improvement revolution across the entire organization. Here are a couple of case studies to that effect.

Case Study: The Cleveland Clinic

Founded in 1921, the Cleveland Clinic has long been a leader in healthcare excellence, in addition to operationally innovating to maintain a lower cost structure. But this wasn't always the case. One of their recent transformations resulted from involving teams like yours in addressing the patient experience, along with the various contributing factors among the internal clinical-care and staff cultures.

Purpose: Despite being repeatedly ranked among the top five U.S. hospitals in *U.S. News & World Report* for overall quality of care and #1 in heart programs, a downward trend in patient satisfaction was noted in the Centers for Medicare & Medicaid Services (CMS) HCAHPS survey. Leadership was concerned that this would quickly result in poor word-of-mouth stories that would undermine not just the clinic's reputation but, more important, the perceived ability to provide care to those patients who may choose to go elsewhere.

Process: The improvement effort began with team leaders like you being introduced to the proven overarching strategy that secures superior results (Chapter 3). Examining surveys and patient feedback, it became apparent that the Cleveland Clinic experience was influenced by more than just the clinical outcomes. The various metrics made it clear that all employees, from administrators to dietary to janitors, made an impression on the patient experience. Therefore, all employees of the Cleveland Clinic were soon considered "caregivers" and encouraged to seek out ways to enhance care in every aspect of their functional role.

The first step was to ensure that every functional team had tools to better understand those they serve (Chapter 8), including ways to assess individual personality traits and the deeper, emotional needs that drive their decision making and satisfaction levels.

In addition, these same tools successfully enhanced the teams' ability to work more effectively together. They also provided guidance for teams to help compassionately manage expectations and interpersonal engagement throughout the patient experience.

Soon, the improvement initiative expanded to environmental and process-oriented aspects of the patient experience. They reimagined wayfinding signage and invested in low-cost solutions to help patients and their families navigate the different buildings with less confusion. In addition, various teams worked together to streamline frustration points, such as making appointments and providing clear discharge instructions.

To drive meaningful improvements, teams began coordinating to establish a "voice of the patient" as well as employee advisory councils to help identify and respond quickly to trending issues before they could develop into larger, systemic problems that might ultimately affect the patient experience, in an initiative they named "Managing the 360." This was driven by an incident involving a standard colorectal-surgery patient, who noted that she interacted with eight physicians, 60 nurses, and a large assortment of phlebotomists, food workers, environmental-services workers, transporters, and so on.

Among the more vital issues was communication. The patients expected to be kept up-to-date using verbiage that they could understand, even amid feelings of anxiety and discomfort. One breakthrough in understanding the feedback was realizing how many patients, or their families, would interpret various aspects of their experience. If they noticed that an area was messy, they translated that as the clinical team not caring, having poor attention to detail, or likely to provide substandard care. Furthermore, the teams discovered that patients would often interpret employees working together and not being cordial to one another as either they weren't happy with the patient or there was bad news that they were not being told. Regardless, the teams realized they needed to take patients' perceptions into consideration when interacting with them to optimize their outcomes.

The clinic even created a Best Practices Department to aid in the sharing of relevant improvements across functions; many of these improvements develop into pilot projects that can expand throughout the larger organization for multiplied benefits. One was establishing weekly huddles among critical floor leaders to address real-time patient and staff concerns. Another was launching "caregiver celebrations," which give managers and frontline workers the opportunity to recognize colleagues who have demonstrated exceptional care for the patients or the organization.

Payoff: After three years of implementing team and overall organizational improvements, the Cleveland Clinic dramatically improved their reputation for patient satisfaction and referrals—elevating their CMS-survey results significantly to the top 8 percent of more than 4,600 hospitals. Overall positive employee satisfaction ratings hit 92 percent. Interfunctional team productivity achieved record highs. The Cleveland Clinic earned top honors regarding their quality and safety results in the University HealthSystem Consortium rankings, out of 97 academic medical centers. Within the first year of creating a single phone number for booking appointments and training centralized schedulers to engage callers more effectively (a process developed by frontline teams), visits by new patients rose a whopping 20 percent! To date, Cleveland Clinic's same-day appointments account for more than 1 million patient visits a year!

Ponder: These large-scale results are a direct consequence of teams getting involved (with the right tools—included in this book) and instituting low- and no-cost improvements that were systematically coordinated to scale throughout the larger organization. What impact could these kinds of improvements have on your healthcare organization?

Case Study: Johnson & Johnson

Johnson & Johnson, the world's largest and most comprehensive manufacturer of healthcare products, is one of only five companies that has been in the top 50 across 52 industries of the Fortune Best Companies rankings since they began, in 1999. The most-admired company in the pharmaceutical industry for the 10th consecutive year, Johnson & Johnson is known for developing innovative solutions to the world's most pressing healthcare needs, such as treatments for deadly diseases, and for improving environmental health.

While Johnson & Johnson has been successful for many years, they experienced a breakthrough transformation recently by challenging their company-wide teams to engage one another and those they serve more fully to optimize their collective potential.

Purpose: Because of the decentralization of Johnson & Johnson's almost 200 operating companies, there was a concern that continued growth would magnify misalignments among the various operations. The strength of the overall corporation depended on each functional team being in full alignment with the others. This required more robust team growth while sharing common tools that allowed for superior orchestration of their collective innovations.

Process: The initiative began with a task force of frontline leaders, who, with the participation of frontline team members, developed six key objectives:

1. Build on Johnson & Johnson core strengths: All team activities need to align with the overarching mission to maintain operational integrity.
2. Make it globally applicable: Because the company's markets are international (47 percent of sales are outside the U.S.), any new developments need to be embraced globally.

3. Make it situationally adaptable: The new approach must allow for dynamic and situational application, so all team leaders can address issues in a relevant way.
4. Make it simple, but not simplistic: The team tools need to be simple enough to be consistently implemented yet sophisticated enough to be effective in their leading-edge scientific environment.
5. Focus on positively changing the behavior of current and future leaders: The only way to grow the organization is to grow the teams, by growing the leadership within those teams.
6. Make it a central part of the Johnson & Johnson leadership-development process: In addition to growing the team and individual team-leader capabilities, the effort must elevate leadership at all levels of the organization, in relation to outcomes.

The process included providing personal assessments of all team leaders (Chapter 4), then follow-up meetings with bosses to determine strengths and gaps for each team leader. After time to prepare, team leaders then engaged their respective teams with tools to reinforce the teams' connection to the Johnson & Johnson mission, vision, and values (Chapter 5)—all in service of unifying team efforts to identify low- and no-cost improvements (Chapters 6 and 8) at the team operations level. This was referred to as "action learning."

The next phase was establishing transparent and timely feedback (Chapter 7), first among the team, then across teams. Each team leader, and then the rest of the team, was held accountable for common standards:

- Living the Johnson & Johnson non-negotiables
- Focusing on the customer and the marketplace
- Encouraging innovation
- Building interdependent partnerships
- Mastering complexity
- Developing self, others, and the organization

Next, each team began by addressing issues that could be improved within their functional operation. Once these team improvements were implemented, the scope of the improvement efforts began to expand to include other teams within their respective departments, then divisions, then across the entire organization. Recent updates included "improving the process of improving," which led to fine-tuning operational potential and resource savings into large-scale reinvestments in product development, cultural workforce enhancements, and profits to investors.

Payoff: The results of these team enhancement efforts were considerable. Overall effectiveness ratings of team leaders increased 72 percent, which influenced overall team effectiveness to improve by 60 percent—creating significant reduction in expenses and top-line growth of more than 30 percent. That said, the overall advantages identified by Johnson & Johnson include more than revenue generation. Here is a brief overview of their stated benefits:

- Enhanced buy-in and team problem solving: Defining the business issues regarding specific improvements for the customer and employee experience increases involvement, which leads to increased buy-in
- Sustained enthusiasm and energy driving change: Creating urgency in decision making keeps progress changes front of mind, rather than the "old" ways of thinking, leading to fresh solutions and team-generated excitement
- Improved planning and attention to follow-up inter-team events: Building in mutual accountability and coordinating frequent feedback helps adjust coordination efforts most effectively throughout the process
- More thorough discussions of issues within and across teams: Developing a culture of emotional safety and constant orientation to the core non-negotiables (Chapter 5) helps guide teams toward root-cause issues and long-term solutions.

Ponder: Do you see misalignment as a problem that needs to be improved to reduce team errors or missed opportunities to provide superior care? If so, how can clarifying your values and mission regarding your team function help drive alignment and improved unity? What ways can you better role-model your values? How can you get more creative to appropriately (and in a low- or no-cost way) enhance your employee or patient experience to create superior value?

"I attribute my success to this—I never gave or took any excuse."

— Florence Nightingale

Finally Beginning Your Breakthrough

My hope is that you can become the catalyst for a success story like these case studies. Every successful large transformation effort is the result of team transformation. No matter if your goals are a series of small improvements or a big shift in how your team operates, the tools in this book are scalable. Focus first on becoming better. Once you master that, you will naturally grow your influence and impact.

Before I introduce a final implementation rollout checklist, you may benefit from some final insights and tools. Let's start with a quick review.

Your perspective as the leader is vital to orchestrating the many moving pieces of this process. Keep the World-Class Success Chain in mind as you manage the timing of your effort. Begin by preparing yourself, as you need to better understand the details of the fantastic improvement that your team is about to create. First, you must examine yourself and take the first steps to improve your own ability to role-model the behaviors you will expect of your team to succeed. You don't have to be perfect, but you need to at least begin this work yourself. Remember, you will be doing more than just telling the way; you'll be *showing* it!

Once you feel 80 percent ready, initiate the tools in this book to prepare your team for success. They need to have confidence that you have a good grasp on the circumstances, that your plan (based on the best practices of world-class organizations) is sound, that they will be involved in ensuring that the decisions made throughout will be relevant and practical, and that you have their back! Even if they understand the logic of the approach, they won't fully buy in until they are emotionally comfortable with it. Support and guide them through that initial fear and you will not only help get them on board, but establish a deeper, more engaged working relationship with them.

One of the most common challenges that team leaders face is when people—either colleagues or patients—assume the worst. The cure for this is the oft-mentioned "communication." The most effective practitioners focus on the foundational work of:

1. Making it simple. If it is too complicated, they won't remember it. Distill the critically important information down to its essence so it is both understandable and memorable.
2. Repetition. Repeating an important message indicates that it is important. Repeating the information they need to know and repeating the context repeats the benefits of that information. Did I mention that repeating the message is important? Repetition can seem repetitive, but it ensures that the message you are repeating repeats in their minds repeatedly. (Should I repeat this?)

Finally, ensure that your collective efforts to improve always remain focused on those you serve (the patient's care is your mission), by way of improved team engagement and the effective use of resources. If you consistently exceed expectations—even a little bit—at each step of the patient and team experience, you will set the stage for a continuous improvement culture that will *never* go out of style.

Figure 9-1. World-Class Success Chain

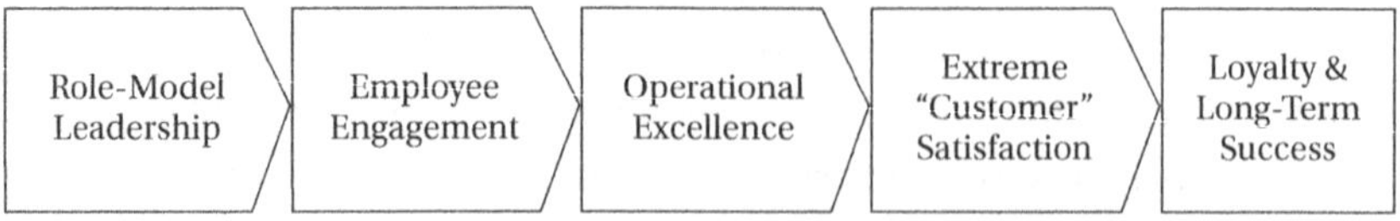

"The capacity to learn is a gift; the ability to learn is a skill; the willingness to learn is a choice."

– Brian Herbert

Building a Case for Buy-In and Support

To get support from your team and anyone else involved with your planned improvement effort, you'll need to "prepare the soil so the seeds can take root." Here are some actions to incorporate as you make those preparations:

- Many people in healthcare tend to insist on "proving" before acting, the result of extensive academic study. Gather whatever relevant evidence you have at hand, but realize that this is often a weapon to use against the intimidating change request. In real life, not everything can be unquestionably "proved" in advance; the goal is *improve* rather than *prove*. Nurture a bias for "action learning" instead.
- Spotlight shortfalls regarding your mission and the experience of those involved—both the patient and the care providers. Here are some actions to consider:
    - Collect feedback from dissatisfied patients, colleagues, and operational partners with specific reactions from previous experiences.
    - Collect data from metrics gathered (from your organization's HR or audit or feedback department) and note the trends and patterns that support taking action.
- The situation: Your team will "know" where things are as far as the day-to-day operation, but it may be enlightening to know about other details related to your circumstances, both inside and outside your organization's walls.
    - Collect data about your healthcare organization's performance, the market, the economy, and your competition, pointing out trends and patterns that indicate where things are likely to move soon.

    - Provide data that clearly indicate the risk and consequences of *not* changing, including direct connections to whatever team members value about being a healthcare professional (include insights from the five essential needs tool), as well as to their personal commitment to providing care that makes the difference they always wanted to make.
- The benefits: Showcase, in a personal, emotionally connected way ("Imagine how it could feel to ..."), the expected benefits of implementing low- and no-cost solutions for:
    - Your patients and their families
    - The team
    - The overall organization (time, resources, budget)

Take some time to fine-tune your message. And keep the message brief—just a minute or two. Think of it as a commercial to persuade them to act. This often helps to frame communication in an efficient, yet impactful way.

"Start by doing what's necessary; then do what's possible; and suddenly, you are doing the impossible."

— Francis of Assisi

Developing Better Habits Requires Nurturing

Anytime we attempt to develop a better way of living, it requires that we stop doing the old, suboptimal approach and create a new, better one.

This has been a challenging juggling act for all of human history, so it won't be easy. You need to approach it differently from the stereotypical New Year's resolution that gets broken in the first couple of weeks—lost in the hectic fog of other demands on your attention. This is often because most "resolutions" are not a reflection of real resolve; they are just superficial wishful thinking. You deserve better. The superior solution is to start with a well-thought-out personal plan and consistently refer to it for recalibration as you will your way to success.

Here's a simple, low-tech approach that has proven to work on an individual or team basis.

Step One: Write a detailed list of descriptions for up to three priority goals that you have (not too many, as it will become overwhelming). There are different ways of thinking about how many new changes to attempt at one time. Some people fare better when they limit themselves to working on one new habit at a time; then, once the new behavior has become habitual, they move to developing the next new habit. I encourage you to begin by writing your goals up like an after-action report, as if you had already accomplished the task. Be as specific as possible to paint as clear a picture of your future as possible—not for some mystical New Age reason, but to make it tangible enough that you can envision the accomplishment. This is an important step. The more thoroughly you can envision the worthwhile goal, the more you can mentally and emotionally engage with it. This will become even more valuable when it comes to time to compel others in the effort to accomplish that goal!

PRO TIP

When aiming for a particular metric, always add the words "*or better*", as in "improve 2 percent *or better*". This prevents you from subconsciously aiming for the lower end of your effort and frees you to strive for bigger achievements than you may have originally considered.

Step Two: Identify your current circumstances and abilities regarding that behavior—particularly what is reinforcing your current, "pre-improvement" behaviors. It is just as important to stop feeding the less healthy behaviors as it is to initiate and feed the new, preferred habit. Again, more clarity leads to insights and stronger motivation to fuel the improvement effort.

PRO TIP

Seek out anyone who understands why a particular practice was instituted for your function. Insist on digging to the root reason, rather than "It was better" or "That's what leadership demanded." The classic Five Whys approach of asking "Why?" after the first four answers to get to the root cause can be an effective (albeit potentially irritating) action.

Step Three: Analyze where you are and where you want to be, then plan manageable actions to bridge that gap. Studies indicate that it takes 30-90 days to go from an initial routine to an established habit: "A habit is a behavior done with little or no thought, while a routine involves a series of behaviors frequently, and intentionally, repeated. A behavior has to be a regularly performed routine before it can become a habit at all."[56] Of course, an enjoyable habit, like eating candy after every meal, obviously develops faster than exercising every day, which requires discomfort, despite the superior benefit. Also, include what obstacles could pose a challenge at each step, so you can proactively remove them before you proceed. Consider what has prevented you from establishing this good habit in the past. The clearer you are about the circumstances affecting this behavior, the more likely you'll be to overcome the real problem and begin a better trajectory for your life.

PRO TIP

A common part of failing to establish a good habit is not having the time to do it effectively. Circumvent this by first going through the time-management tool in Chapter 7 to create a more conducive environment to support your effort.

[56] DePaul, 2021.

Step Four: Take action. Any step, even a small one, is a win toward making progress. Don't wait for some magical courage to bubble up and energize you. Courage always comes as a *by-product* of success, and success always comes from *doing*. Consider it a muscle that grows as you challenge and use it. The *journey* is what generates encouragement, inspiration, and commitment. You must prime the pump by taking the first few steps, then establish the discipline to continue the adventure to your improved future.

PRO TIP

What "nudges" can you design into your plan? Accountability partners at key times? It's helpful to connect the desired new behavior with an existing routine.[57] Link the new behavior with a more enjoyable one. For example: To start working out on the treadmill, commit to listening to your favorite podcast only while doing so. Do the enjoyable activity only in tandem with the new behavior.

Step Five: Design regular reminders as reinforcement. Your typical workday is probably hectic, so it's easy to get caught up in the swirl of dealing with all that. One effective solution is to start and end each day by reviewing your plan. Reviewing at the start of the day helps remind you of your higher-level goal and incorporate it into the details of your day. Reviewing at the end of the day allows you to reflect on how well the new effort is going and make any adjustments. This feedback is important to the inevitable testing and adjusting that comes with launching any improvement effort. Consider this: If you were driving your car in your neighborhood and all the windows were covered, would you rather have constructive feedback every two seconds or every minute? The more immediate the feedback, the faster you adjust, and the more quickly you get on the best path to success.

[57] Milkman et al., 2014.

PRO TIP

Make your goal and behavior commitment your phone's lock screen. Every time you go to open your phone, you'll be reminded of your intended new habit and why you should care.

Step Six: Reinforce progress by celebrating successes. All your current habit behaviors and routines are the natural consequence of some kind of reinforcement. Sometimes, the reinforcement that started the habit no longer exists, yet the habit has continued. To cement in the habit (for as long as it's healthy), spotlight the behavior and associated benefit to reinforce the behavior being repeated. The better habits you fill your life with, the more beneficial consequences you will enjoy. The sooner you start, the earlier you will reap the benefits.

PRO TIP

For team application, if possible, acknowledge the success of any member of your team in front of the team, so you can showcase the benefit to those you serve as well as the benefit to the team. It's also a nice opportunity to remind them that the improvement idea came from them and to "keep *your* ideas flowing so we can continue making a better difference and enjoy more benefits."

"Most of the important things in the world have been accomplished by people who have kept on trying when there seemed to be no hope at all."

– Dale Carnegie

Expect and Resist Resistance

As you begin your implementation efforts, keep in mind that every attempt at improving new ideas will face natural resistance. People will be fearful (as I mentioned in Chapter 2) but lean on your compassion to help them feel safer. Expect that you and your team will fall short occasionally as you try new things—but that is merely part of the process. Help them understand this and manage their expectations. Have confidence in your collective abilities to figure out what needs to happen during the inevitable twists and turns of your process. Keep at it until you break through.

Think of it this way: When a football team executes the first play and they gain no yards, do they just remove their helmets, walk off the field, and leave the game? Of course not! They know that one play does not determine the outcome of the game. They understand that not every play will work according to plan—but, thankfully, not every play is necessary for long-term success. Success is the natural consequence of a series of imperfect efforts that build on one another to create a pattern of dependable outcomes that get progressively better over time. Your responsibility as the team leader is to influence this effort.

That said, when resistance arises, and it will, address it. It won't magically go away on its own. Invite team members to air their concerns. Listen. Listen some more. You can't deal with their resistance until you fully understand it—and them. Pushback is often an indicator that you haven't connected with them enough. And you won't earn legitimate buy-in until you address their concerns enough for them to trust you during the initial steps to test your idea out, which is a fantastic excuse for them to be involved. As is often said, "If they aren't part of the solution, they will be part of the problem!"

Pushback is often an indicator that you haven't connected with them enough.

One final insight about dealing with those haters who refuse to even consider improving: If you've repeatedly done your best to engage them on a direct and personal basis and they still have no intention of joining in, *stop trying*. Or as noted researcher Brené Brown refreshingly once said, "Don't try to win over the haters; you are not a jackass whisperer." Invest your efforts where they will best benefit the team. (And hold the haters accountable.)

You're reading this book now because you need to start now. Table 9-1 is a tool to help you document your improvement plan:

Table 9-1. Strategic Team Leader Improvement Plan

Strategic Team Leader Improvement Plan						
	Goal 1		Goal 2		Goal 3	
Detailed Description						
Current Circumstances						
Perceived Gap						
Reinforcing Old?						
Reinforcing New?						
Possible Obstacles?						
Strategies to Overcome						
Accountability Partner						
Launch Date						
Milestones	Milestone	Reward	Milestone	Reward	Milestone	Reward
Date:						
Date:						
Date:						
Date:						
Date:						

Your world may change without your involvement, but it will not likely be the improvement you know is possible. You are reading this book right now because you want to make a difference.

But merely wanting that isn't enough. You need to engage others who want to make a difference as well.

But sadly, that isn't enough either. You need to align your collective behaviors to make a difference.

Again, that just isn't enough. You must act. *That* is the only thing that ultimately makes a difference.

> *"What good is an idea if it remains an idea? Try. Experiment. Iterate. Fail. Try again. Change the world."*
>
> **— Simon Sinek**

Final Thoughts, Part Two: Starting Your Transformation: What to Do *Now*

Don't make the mistake of finishing this book and passively hoping that things get better. The examples, insights, and tools I've shared are only information. As entrepreneur Derek Sivers has quipped, "If more information were the answer, we'd all be billionaires with six-pack abs." Improvement happens only when someone *starts*. I've found that, in nearly all circumstances, the obstacle stopping most people is ... starting. Take the first step!

If you really want to make a difference in your real world, know that the smallest deed is more valuable than the greatest intention. When you blend the courage to begin with the discipline to persevere, success is just a matter of time.

Merely talking about change is not going to change anything.

It only takes one person to make a difference. Be that person! That time *is now.* Merely talking about change is not going to change anything. You now have access to all the tools—you simply need to take the first steps to bring them to life.

We all struggle with making time when our workload is already overwhelming. Unfortunately, not having the time to start improvements that desperately need to happen is *not* a valid excuse. We all have the same 24 hours in a day. The real issue is how we manage the time that we have—and that is all about priorities. Consider this: There are other people, likely in your organization, maybe even in your functional area, who seem to get more done in the same timeframe. Reach out to them and learn how they juggle the many, constantly shifting issues that flare up in your particular healthcare environment. Approach your leader with the request to support your new efforts to improve your team results. Confidently seize the reality that each successful behavior is being implemented by someone else, so it can be done by you and your team.

We each experience the natural consequences of what we do or don't do. If you want better outcomes, then change your behaviors to those that naturally lead to those better results.

The steps in Figure 9-1 are the catalyst for an exciting journey of improvement that will be the turnaround point; everyone will look back to it and know that's where the new chapter began.

Figure 9-2. Continuous Improvement Implementation Process

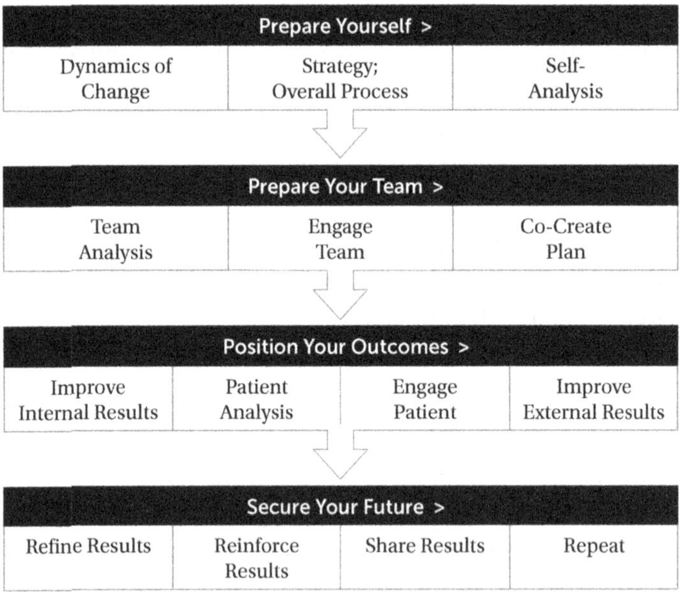

"You just begin. You solve one problem, then you solve the next problem, and soon, if you solve enough of them, you get to come home."

— Mark Watney, The Martian

Your Team Transformation Checklist

Life is an ever-changing three-dimensional experience, so no two-dimensional implementation plan in a static book will ever match your circumstances perfectly. That said, I'm offering this checklist as the chronological order that seems to get the best results most often—it helps you build insights, capabilities, and momentum effectively, each from the preceding step. Rearrange things if your circumstances warrant—the most important approach is the one that works best for you and your team. Also, don't let this list intimidate you. Simply start each one as you get to it and keep going!

Prepare Yourself

It is vital that you get yourself ready first so you can most effectively lead your team. Remember, you don't have to be perfect—just competent. Your goal is to develop your ability to model effective relationship and operational behaviors, then anticipate the improvement process and team dynamics that will follow. Here are the steps that will set you up for success:

1. Go to **ResultsStat.com/BookResources** and download the *free* worksheets for targeting your personal efforts.
2. Complete the leader assessment (Chapter 4). Evaluate your current skill set and begin efforts to improve those skills most needed for you, your team, and your patients.
3. Develop your case for implementation (Chapter 4) to most effectively articulate your approach to practically improve things for your team, your patients/clients, and your organization.
4. Identify what drains and energizes you (Chapter 6) to begin balancing your life.
5. Complete the fear analysis (Chapter 2) to help you understand what has been affecting you, your colleagues, and those you serve so you can better support their experiences.
6. Fill out the influence tool (Chapter 4) to leverage those who can help support your efforts.

7. Complete the personality trait tool (Chapter 8, full assessment in free online workbook) to gain insights about your preferred styles of communication. You can also begin exploring how your team members' personalities affect how they work together.
8. Develop your draft team mission, vision, and values (Chapter 5) as a starting place to clarify and align your team non-negotiables. This will prepare you for introducing this tool to your team later.
9. Complete your Team-Leader Alignment tool (Chapter 6, expanded tool in online workbook) to prepare your efforts to get you and your team more aligned with one another's behavioral preferences.
10. Work out the time management tool (Chapter 7) to improve how you manage your time as well as familiarize yourself with the tool so you can facilitate your team's use later.
11. Approach your boss and get their support for your upcoming efforts.
12. Engage accountability/support partners (at minimum, a colleague and your boss) who share your hopes for a better workplace and are willing to support your efforts. (Bonus points for an influential senior leader whom you make aware of your efforts to improve the team/organization!)

Prepare Your Team

In addition to setting yourself up for success, effectively lay the groundwork to make the improvement effort as engaging for your team as possible. Here are some actions to consider:

13. Meet with an influential team member(s) to share improvement goals and book insights (share a summary—available on website) and gather their insights and feedback.
14. Finalize plans for a rollout of the team improvement initiative.
15. Communicate the improvement effort launch.

16. Collectively complete the leader-team alignment questions (Chapter 6, expanded tool in online workbook); use the document or select certain questions.
17. Discuss each question for insights about each team member's preferences and enhanced understanding of where everyone is coming from.
18. Collectively complete the personality trait tool (Chapter 8, full assessment in online workbook) and discuss.
19. Collectively complete the team version of your organizational mission, vision, and values (Chapter 5)—include behaviors that best bring the values to life for your functional team.
20. Brainstorm your team's continue/stop/start lists (Chapter 6) and prioritize them for action plans.
21. Conduct the team skills audit (Chapter 6) to identify and bridge skills gaps.
22. Conduct the team weaver (Chapter 6) to identify and support relational and results improvements.
23. Review the five essential needs (Chapter 8) and identify the needs of your team and patients/clients.
24. Begin enhanced weekly team meetings. Prime the discussion with targeted questions such as:
    - How are we each feeling about the improvement process?
    - What accomplishments have we made so far?
    - What have we learned since our last check-in?
    - What issues or challenges have we encountered?
    - Who needs what support?
    - Any new low- or no-cost solutions or insights?
    - What are our next priorities? Goals? Plans?
    - Any potential obstacles?
    - Who is doing what by when?

    Then remind them about the purpose of this (temporarily uncomfortable) effort: to become the team that achieves the results you all can be proud of!

25. Begin an enhanced daily team briefing, to include recognitions and celebrations, key success tips, daily operations update, development tips or insights, and requests for feedback or involvement regarding improvement efforts.

Position Your Outcomes

This part of the rollout often overlaps with the others, depending on the unique needs of your team's circumstances. These steps emphasize the results aspect of your improvement:

26. Complete the Patient Experience Sequence (Chapter 7) to identify details that matter most to your patients and initiate improvements.
27. Complete your Team Experience Sequence (Chapter 7) to identify details that matter most to your team and initiate improvements.
28. Prioritize improvement projects for the most effective roll-out.
29. Post a tracking sheet and document progress. Schedule hard commitments every day, no matter how small the action, to generate legitimate momentum toward your team's most important goals. Post (if possible, out of patient view) the issue, goal, responsibilities, and metrics so the entire team sees progress.
30. Coordinate with other team leaders to streamline and optimize handoffs.

Secure Your Future

This phase reinforces ongoing improvements and supports future efforts.

31. Elevate progress and learnings monthly to targeted leadership.
32. Schedule regular report-outs (written or in-person) with your boss and any higher-level leader who is a shareholder in the issue(s) you are committed to improving. Gather feedback on how you can best continue to contribute to your team,

department, division, or organization.

33. Revisit key patient- and team-experience issues as needed.
34. Identify new improvement opportunities as circumstances evolve.

"Legacy is not leaving something for people. It's leaving something in people."

– Peter Strople

Final Thoughts, Part Three

So, you've discovered the behind-the-scenes implementation secrets that earn extraordinary results for world-class teams. You now have the proven tools needed to achieve the future you've always hoped for, but ... you have to *start.*

As famed writer and mountaineer William Hutchison Murray once wrote:

> Until one is committed, there is hesitancy, the chance to draw back, always ineffectiveness. Concerning all acts of initiative and creation, there is one elementary truth, the ignorance of which kills countless ideas and splendid plans: that the moment one definitely commits oneself, then providence moves too. All sorts of things occur to help one that would never otherwise have occurred. A whole stream of events issues from the decision, raising in one's favour all manner of unforeseen incidents, meetings, and material assistance which no man could have dreamed would have come his way. Whatever you can do or dream you can, begin it. Boldness has genius, power and magic in it. Begin it now.

The time for merely thinking or talking about starting your improvement is done. It's time to commit and put your hopes and dreams into action.

Once you have an idea of what you think could improve things, take action within 24 hours—or you'll lose momentum. Take advantage of the surge of adventure-facing energy that wells up in you when you are inspired to make a difference. Don't let that catalyst die, like so many missed opportunities in the past. You know how it feels to regret not doing something good when you had the chance. Make this opportunity different!

It's time to commit and put your hopes and dreams into action.

Momentum comes from consistent behaviors over a sustained period, which generates team confidence and buy-in—and results. Keep learning and taking action—even small steps—each and every day. *Consistency* on what matters most is what eventually achieves extraordinary results.

"Do not wait; the time will never be 'just right.' Start where you stand, and work with whatever tools you may have at your command, and better tools will be found as you go along."

– George Herbert

Don't let your fear of the unknown prevent you from starting. Your passion for delivering the care your patients (and team) need is far more important.

Don't let your colleagues prevent you from starting. They are simply scarred from previous failures. Your compassion and care will protect them and encourage them to realize their dream.

Don't let temporary barriers prevent you from starting. You can identify alternative routes as you study the circumstances—adjust and improve.

Starting is always the most difficult step in the process. Choose to trust your ability to learn, adapt, and overcome—forging your capability, strength, and resilience as a consequence of the *effort.*

Not only will your immediate working conditions improve, but who you (and your team) become as a result of this effort will enhance the rest of your life in countless ways.

This is the way to thrive in life. The sooner you start, the faster (and longer) you'll enjoy the benefits.

If you don't invest the time and effort to create the career that you want, you'll be forced to waste a lot of time and effort dealing with a career you *don't* want. I could share silly motivational memes, or dozens of inspiring before and after examples, or quote from as many brilliant authors as you can tolerate, but until your desire to succeed overcomes your willingness to settle, you and those around you will continue to needlessly suffer.

And frankly, you, and those you care about, deserve better than that.

Improving your part of the healthcare world is possible and needed *now*.

You want things to improve. People who count on you need it to improve.

You have this opportunity—and now you have the proven tools to finally realize your potential.

So, for your sake, and those you care about—start.

Now.

Reminder

For your *free* workbook download, in a larger, more user-friendly format, just visit **ResultsStat.com/BookResources** or use this QR code for your convenience:

Afterward

This is the end of the book, but if you implement the various tools inside, it can be the beginning of your new chapter—make it the best chapter of your career! Your breakthrough(s) are on the other side of your first step. *Start now!*

I trust that this book has provided you with helpful insights and implementation tools that will make your healthcare world more impactful. In addition to the downloadable worksheets from the content, please feel free to check out **ResultsStat.com/Resources** for additional resources that I will continue adding in the coming years.

And I have a personal favor to ask you: Would you mind taking a quick minute to post a review of this book on Amazon or on the ResultsStat.com website? It will cost you nothing but mean the world to me if you could help bring it to the attention of others who need the insights and tools to improve their team and their patient care. Thank you for paying it forward!

Also, my hope is that you reach out to me to share success stories, feedback, and/or questions. I am a resource for you outside the pages of this book. Email me directly at **Mark@ResultsStat.com** and I will be pleased to help you any way I can. (And if you feel this book was helpful in your quest to improve your outcomes, I would be *extremely* grateful if you recommended it to others in your organization. Thank you so much in advance!)

Finally, if your healthcare organization wants to initiate any kind of leadership or organizational improvement effort, I would be honored to help set you up for success. Just contact me at **ResultsStat.com/Contact** and I'll be happy to send you any additional information or even schedule a no-cost, no-obligation call to discuss your circumstances and goals.

Looking forward,

Mark

References

The following is my list of citations referenced in this book. Despite my best intentions, I expect that I may have made a mistake somewhere in this book. If you happen to notice anything that is misattributed or not giving credit where it is due, please contact me at **Mark@ResultsStat.com** so I can correct the issue as soon as possible. (Thank you for your attention to detail!)

1. *Murthy, V. 2022. Addressing Health Worker Burnout: The U.S. Surgeon General's Advisory on Building a Thriving Health Workforce.* https://www.hhs.gov/sites/default/files/health-worker-wellbeing-advisory.pdf.
2. National Institute for Occupational Safety and Health (NIOSH). 2018. "Healthcare Workers and Work Stress." Accessed June 21, 2023. www.cdc.gov/niosh/topics/healthcare/workstress.html.
3. Rotenstein, L.S., R. Brown, C. Sinsky, and M. Linzer. 2023. "The Association of Work Overload With Burnout and Intent to Leave the Job Across the Healthcare Workforce During COVID-19." *Journal of General Internal Medicine* 38(8): 1920–27. www.ncbi.nlm.nih.gov/pmc/articles/PMC10035977/.
4. Bird, A., T. Lichtenau, and D. Michels. 2016. "The What, Who and How of Delivering Results." Bain & Company, February 9. www.bain.com/insights/what-who-and-how-of-delivering-results/.
5. Hiatt, J. 2006. *ADKAR: A Model for Change in Business, Government and Our Community.* Fort Collins, CO: Prosci.
6. Dowling, M. 2017. "Michael Dowling: 4 Most Important Healthcare Trends in 2018." *Becker's Hospital Review,* December 18. www.beckershospitalreview.com/hospital-management-administration/michael-dowling-4-most-important-healthcare-trends-in-2018.html.
7. Reichheld, F. 1993. "Loyalty-Based Management." *Harvard Business Review,* March–April. https://hbr.org/1993/03/loyalty-based-management.
8. Schneid, J. 2019. Conversation with author, February.
9. Sikka, R., J.M. Morath, and L. Leape. 2015. "The Quadruple Aim: Care, Health, Cost and Meaning in Work." *BMJ Quality & Safety* 24(10): 608–10. https://pubmed.ncbi.nlm.nih.gov/26038586/.
10. Wolf, J.A. 2018. "The Consumer Has Spoken: Patient Experience Is Now Healthcare's Core Differentiator." *Patient Experience Journal* 5(1): 1–4. https://pxjournal.org/journal/vol5/iss1/1/.

11. Temkin, B., M. Dorsey, and T. Quaadgras. 2022. *Global Study: ROI of Customer Experience, 2022.* Provo, UT: Qualtrics XM. www.xminstitute.com/research/global-roi-customer-experience-2022/.
12. Centers for Medicare & Medicaid Services (CMS). 2008. "HCAHPS Facts." www.cms.gov/newsroom/fact-sheets/hcahps-facts.
13. Sanborn, M. 2006. *You Don't Need a Title to Be a Leader: How Anyone, Anywhere, Can Make a Positive Difference.* New York: Crown Currency.
14. Calloway, J. 2019. *The Leadership Mindset: How Today's Successful Business Leaders Think.* Cedar Circle Publishing.
15. Harris, D., Discussion with author, 2019.
16. Montini, 2014. "Las Vegas Downtown Project Loses Tony Hsieh as Its Leader." *Inc.*, September 30. www.inc.com/laura-montini/zappos-ceo-tony-hsieh-step-down-las-vegas-downtown-project.html.
17. Microsoft News Center. 2016. "Microsoft to Acquire LinkedIn." https://news.microsoft.com/2016/06/13/microsoft-to-acquire-linkedin/#sm.00000xf0tlfww5fb5z563cqox5d80.
18. Iger, R. 2019. *The Ride of a Lifetime: Lessons Learned From 15 Years as CEO of the Walt Disney Company.* New York: Random House.
19. Schwartz, B. 2015a. "What's the Most Satisfying Job in the World? You'd Be Surprised." *Ideas.Ted.Com*, September 8. https://ideas.ted.com/whats-the-most-satisfying-job-in-the-world-youd-be-surprised/.
20. Schwartz, B. 2015b. *Why We Work.* New York: Simon & Schuster/TED.
21. Pope Francis, 2018. "Address of His Holiness Pope Francis to Members of the Italian Federation of the Boards of Nursing Professions (FNOPI)." www.vatican.va/content/francesco/en/speeches/2018/march/documents/papa-francesco_20180303_ipasvi.html.
22. Senge, P.M. 2006. *The Fifth Discipline.* New York: Doubleday.
23. Mullaney, T. 2017. "5 Key Business Lessons From Amazon's Jeff Bezos." CNBC, January 12. www.cnbc.com/2016/05/13/5-key-business-lessons-from-amazons-jeff-bezos.html.
24. Weiner, J. (@jeffweiner). 2017. "Big misconception about managing compassionately is that it's a 'soft' skill. Most compassionate people I know are typically the strongest." Twitter post, October 6.
25. Yohn, D.L. 2018. *Fusion: How Integrating Brand and Culture Powers the World's Greatest Companies.* Boston: Nicholas Brealey.
26. Rosenthal, S. 2018. Conversation with the author, December 30.
27. Mahoney, M. 2020. "Culture 500: Introducing the 2020 Culture Champions",

MITSloan Management Review, October 13. https://sloanreview.mit.edu/projects/culture-500-introducing-the-2020-culture-champions/

28. Ibid.
29. Harter, J. 2024. "In New Workplace, U.S. Employee Engagement Stagnates." Gallup, January 23. www.gallup.com/workplace/608675/new-workplace-employee-engagement-stagnates.aspx.
30. Harter, J. 2020. "4 Factors Driving Record-High Employee Engagement in U.S." Gallup, February 4. www.gallup.com/workplace/284180/factors-driving-record-high-employee-engagement.aspx.
31. Quinn, R., B. Crane, T. Thompson, and R.E. Quinn. 2024. "Why Real-Time Leadership Is So Hard." *Harvard Business Review*, January–February, pp. 56–9.
32. Zaki, J. 2024. "How to Sustain Your Empathy in Difficult Times." *Harvard Business Review*, January–February. https://hbr.org/2024/01/how-to-sustain-your-empathy-in-difficult-times.
33. Plemmons, J. 2018. "2 Remedies for Reducing Burnout Among Healthcare Workers." Gallup, March 13. www.gallup.com/workplace/236132/remedies-reducing-burnout-among-healthcare-workers.aspx.
34. Mayo Clinic Staff. 2023. "Job Burnout: How to Spot It and Take Action." Mayo Clinic, November 30. www.mayoclinic.org/healthy-lifestyle/adult-health/in-depth/burnout/art-20046642.
35. Reichheld, F. 2011. *The Ultimate Question 2.0*. Boston: Harvard Business Review Press.
36. Nigam, J.A.S., R.M. Barker, T.R. Cunningham, N.G. Swanson, and L.C. Chosewood. 2023. "*Vital Signs*: Health Worker—Perceived Working Conditions and Symptoms of Poor Mental Health—Quality of Worklife Survey, United States, 2018–2022. *Morbidity and Mortality Weekly Report* 72(44): 1197–1205.
37. Walters, S. 2022. "How Nurses Can Combat Compassion Fatigue." *NurseJournal*, February 18. https://nursejournal.org/articles/combating-compassion-fatigue-in-nursing/.
38. Ury, W. 2007. *The Power of a Positive No*. New York: Bantam.
39. Berry, L.L., and K.D. Seltman. 2008. *Management Lessons From Mayo Clinic*. New York: McGraw Hill.
40. Hobson, N. 2024. "Satya Nadella's Microsoft Just Became the Most Valued Company in the World. And It's Thanks to Psychology, Not Tech." *Inc.*, January 16. www.inc.com/nick-hobson/satya-nadellas-microsoft-just-became-most-valued-company-in-world-its-thanks-to-psychology-not-tech.html?leadId=169297720.
41. Potter, P., S. Boxerman, L. Wolf, J. Marshall, D. Grayson, J. Sledge, and B. Evanoff. 2004. "Mapping the Nursing Process: A New Approach for

Understanding the Work of Nursing." *Journal of Nursing Administration* 34(2): 101–9.

42. Castellucci, M. 2020. "Yale New Haven's COVID-19 Nurse-Staffing Model Has Long-Term Benefits." *Modern Healthcare*, October 17. www.modernhealthcare.com/care-delivery/yale-new-havens-covid-19-nurse-staffing-model-has-long-term-benefits.
43. Meis, C. 2018. "Jeff Bezos' Rules to Live By." *Success*, July 31. www.success.com/jeff-bezos-rules-to-live-by/.
44. Ibid.
45. Ibid.
46. Perna, G. 2023. "Epic CEO Judy Faulkner Touts Gen AI, Clinical Research Tools." *Modern Healthcare*, December 5. www.modernhealthcare.com/digital-health/epic-ceo-judy-faulkner-generative-ai-athenahealth-forbes-healthcare-summit.
47. Sanborn, M. 2011. *Up, Down, or Sideways*. Carol Stream, IL: Tyndale House.
48. University of Utah Health. 2023. The Five Elements of Patient Experience. September 11. https://accelerate.uofuhealth.utah.edu/improvement/the-five-elements-of-patient-experience.
49. Knight, M. 2019. Conversation with author, October.
50. Ibid.
51. Ibid.
52. de Korne, D.F. 2018. Conversation with the author, October.
53. Colin N. 2018. "People Share the Worst Customer Service Experience They've Ever Had." *Tickld*, January 19. www.tickld.com/social/22wspeople-share-the-worst-customer-service-experience-theyve-ever-had/.
54. Cleveland Clinic. n.d. "Programs and Services." https://my.clevelandclinic.org/departments/patient-experience/depts/office-patient-experience/programs.
55. Jones, M.D., and J.J. Kober. 2019. *Lead With Your Customer: Transforming Culture and Brand Into World-Class Excellence*. 2nd edition. Alexandria, VA: ATD Press.
56. DePaul, K. 2021. "What Does It Really Take to Build a New Habit?" *Harvard Business Review*, February 2. https://hbr.org/2021/02/what-does-it-really-take-to-build-a-new-habit.
57. Milkman, K., J.A. Minson, K.G.M. Volpp. 2014. "Holding the Hunger Games Hostage at the Gym: An Evaluation of Temptation Bundling." *Management Science* 60(2): 283–99. https://pubsonline.informs.org/doi/10.1287/mnsc.2013.1784.

About the Author

While you can download his traditional bio at **ResultsStat.com**, here is a quick exec summary of why clients say Mark has street cred:

Real-World Implementation Experience —

Mark's Disney career spanned 26 years (numerous leadership positions) involving a wide variety of functional roles—from high-profile (Special Events: managing President Reagan's "2nd inauguration") to the lower-profile (Organizational Development, Resorts, Disney Institute), Mark has been hip-deep in Disney strategies and daily operational implementation. (As he likes to say: *"Have I got stories..."*)

Over the past 20 years, Mark has been personally involved with over two dozen Fortune 500 company transformation efforts. The interesting thing? Mark discovered that all the best organizations follow the same path to sustainable success (and he's got all their tools that he's willing to share with your implementation team!)

Dynamic and Engaging Speaking Skills —

Since Mark's first speech (ask him to tell you that incredible story) to his most recent last week, he has delivered over 1,300 keynotes (so far) in 54 countries (so far) on 6 (so far) of the 7 continents in the world. Most of Mark's clients continue to be repeat requests—a fact that he works ridiculously hard to maintain.

And He Has a Passion to Help Your Healthcare Organization —

If you need to improve any aspect of your leadership, employee engagement, operational excellence, or patient satisfaction, Mark would be honored to help. Just go to **ResultsStat.com/Contact** and begin your long-overdue breakthrough!

Made in United States
Orlando, FL
04 November 2026

90207812R00134